The
Capital
of Hope

The
Capital
of Hope

Brasília and Its People

Alex Shoumatoff

Vintage Books
A Division of Random House, Inc.
New York

To Ana and our family in Brazil

FIRST VINTAGE BOOKS EDITION, DECEMBER 1990

Copyright © 1980 by Alex Shoumatoff

Library of Congress Cataloging-in-Publication Data
Shoumatoff, Alex.
The capital of hope / Alex Shoumatoff.
p. cm.
Reprint. Originally published: New York : Coward, McCann &
Geoghegan, 1980.
ISBN 0-679-73326-4 (pbk.)
1. Brasília (Brazil) 2. Brazil—Capital and capitol. I. Title.
F2647.S5 1990
981'.74—dc20   90-50438
CIP

Manufactured in the United States of America
10 9 8 7 6 5 4 3 2 1

Contents

Foreword: In Two Dimensions
by José Aparecido de Oliveira,
Governor of Brasília

vii

Part One

1

Part Two

63

Part Three

117

Epilogue

209

Foreword to the Brazilian Edition: In Two Dimensions

by José Aparecido Oliveira, Governor of Brasília

Among the realities of Brasília, two dimensions stand out: one internal, from the driving force of regional development and national integration; and the other external, as a model and source of inspiration for new urban centers in these times approaching the third millennium.

Alex Shoumatoff's book *The Capital of Hope,* originally published by Coward, McCann and Geoghegan, Inc., of New York, and now being published in Portuguese by Editora Anima, Ltd., of Rio de Janeiro, faithfully portrays those two aspects, less by direct statement than by the deductions which the reader is led to make.

A journalist of vast resources and broad experience with life on the South American subcontinent (and particularly in Brazil) to which he also finds himself linked by family ties, Shoumatoff undertook a task of investigative reportage worthy of the important theme.

Really aimed at the English-speaking public, the work is also of singular interest for Brazilians, because it is so rich and perceptive in the facts, quotations, and episodes it sets forth, some of which have lain dormant in the memory of the very old and most of them unknown to the young.

The seriousness of the investigation and the rigorousness of the information did not induce the author to exceed the bounds of journalism and yield to the temptation of writing an overlabored, sociological work. On the contrary, at times the text assumes the form of a fictional narrative conveyed in the first-person singular.

Parading through the pages of this book are many characters who even today pass through the streets of Brasília and Brazil, as well as several international figures. Among the latter, was the first space hero, Yuri Gagarin, who exclaimed before the city under construction, "I feel as though I have disembarked on another planet, not on earth." Or the emperor of Ethiopia, Haile Selassie, who, in the middle of his visit, amid comic and dramatic occurrences, received the news that he had been deposed by his son. Or the French minister of culture, André Malraux, who in a memorable speech identified Brazil's destiny as that of its new capital, which he called "The Capital of Hope."

Shoumatoff's work goes to the origins of the idea of moving the capital, dwelling on the fifty years compressed into five during which Juscelino Kubitschek, aided by Israel Pinheiro and the artist-builders Lúcio Costa, Oscar Niemeyer, and Burle Marx, founded the monumental city in the wilderness of the central plateau. The work spans the time up to the beginning of the last military administration.

With *The Capital of Hope*, the importance of Brasília increases in the international press. Months ago, Alan Riding's article, entitled "Brazil's Capital: Old-Age Pains at 25," was prominently displayed in the most prestigious United States newspaper, the *New York Times*, and was quickly picked up by the *Herald Tribune*, which circulates in Europe. Louis Wiznitzer also treated the theme in an article in the influential North American newspaper, the *Christian Science Monitor,* under the title "Brasília Moves to Become More Livable." And Charles Vanhecke, in the French daily *Le Monde,* talked about the broad walkway at the edge of the lake in his "Tempête sur un lac" ("Storm on a Lake").

There is a noticeable difference between the North American editions of Shoumatoff's work and the reportage that has appeared in the daily press and the press of late. These last were more up-to-date. For example, Vanhecke dealt with highly emotional subjects, as did Lúcio Costa's beautiful text, which is transcribed here.

> I assume that the inhabitants of the lots on the blocks on the lake are civilized people. The open areas that lead to the edge of the lake were conceived of as green spaces with free access, though in practice for common use by the inhabitants themselves, since the presence there of people who are not residents in the immediate area will always be occasional. Therefore, then, the walkway foreseen in the plan and now being laid will be a simple trail, narrow and curving, preferably paved, on the green, sylvan ground. This is not going to prejudice the legitimate rights of anyone, but, on the contrary, it will offer to whoever lives on the blocks by the lake, and on the internal blocks, long promenades and opportunity for jogging, the upkeep remaining in the charge of the residents themselves who have an interest in the appearance of the back part of their respective lot. They will have, as well, the right to plant whatever they want: fruit-bearing trees (monkey-pots, trumpet creepers, silk-cottons, mangos, flamboyants), shrubs—oleander, croton, clustering acacia, manaca, coco palm, jasmine—or even ground cover that does not need great care, such as briza grass, impatiens, plumbago, and so forth, always retaining the green surface, lawn or field, where children might play, and everyone might be able to relax in his

canvas chair, away from the private area belonging to him, which will be bounded by a "living fence" or a simple wall, preferably whitewashed.

The original volume in English lacked one chapter. And it is being lived by those of us who, in this new, national program initiated by the vigorous leadership of President José Sarney, are claiming Brasília as the seat of the new republic Tancredo Neves proclaimed.

With debate and democratic participation, along with steering the government back to the original plan for the capital, we resume implementation of the integration of the city, as "urbs" and as "civitas." This is the chapter the author decided to add in the current editions in order to bring the book up-to-date.

Translation © Meredith Dodge

Acknowledgments

This book was written over the summer of 1979. The political picture it gives is that of the first months of 1979. The picture has altered considerably since then, brightening along the lines everyone anticipated. I would like to thank many people for their help, especially Manuel Mendes, who opened many doors in Brasília and gave so much of his time and energy; Dr. David Gifford of the University of Brasília, who told me about the butterflies; his student Helen Coles, who told me about the termites; William Shawn and Robert Bingham, who advised me throughout the project and prepared the distilled version that ran in *The New Yorker*.

Part One

Observing a custom of northeastern Brazil, José Leonias buried the umbilical cords of his fourteen children under the cashew tree in front of his house. They were all delivered at home by two old midwives, Dom Dom and Militar, one of whom was black, the other white. The first child, Daniel, came in 1931, and was followed, at roughly twenty-month intervals, by Iraci, Marie José, Waldemar, Mario, Terezinha, Maria de Lourdes, Francisco das Chagas, Tadeu, Antonio Hedevirgem, José Ademir, and Luís Afonso; two others died before they reached ten. The house stood at the corner of two unpaved streets, Ruas Floriano Peixoto and Padre Uchôa, not far from the main square of Floriano, the third-largest city in the state of Piauí. The names of both streets were inscribed on blue plaques on the sides of the building. It was a rambling, one-story grey stucco house with a red tile roof and heavy jacaranda doors and shutters that were thrown open each morning. The rooms had high ceilings and were numerous enough to contain not only the whole family, but the frequent invasions of relatives, a thriving general store, and a small hotel run by José Leonias' wife, Dona Joana Maria de Jesus. He came from a village slightly more than twenty-two miles from Floriano that today is almost entirely populated with his relatives. His grandfather had had sixteen children and eighty-six grandchildren, and had lived to see seventy-two of his great-grandchildren and two of his great-great-grandchildren before dying at a hundred and twenty. They were poor, dark-skinned people like almost everyone in Piauí, subsistence farmers of corn, manioc, and beans with a few head of cattle. Dona Joana's mother had come from Ceará, the next state to the north, during a severe drought. Her father, João Apóstolo de Jesus, was the son of a wild Indian, perhaps a Timbira, who had been captured in his youth and raised by a family of homesteaders called de Jesus. The spread of the de Jesus family tree is almost as impressive as that of the Leonias tree; but in Dona Joana, now in her sixties, the Indian traits, evident in her quiet grace, her straight silver hair, and her deeply wrinkled features, predominate.

The first point about Piauí is that it is blistering hot, close to a hundred degrees most of the year. The second is that it is poor, the most destitute and neglected of Brazil's twenty-two states. If Piauí is the Missouri of Brazil (a reasonable comparison once one has made adjustments for the relative economic levels of the two countries), then Floriano is its Joplin. Floriano grew up early in the last century on the right bank of the silent, glassy, and treacherously swift Parnaíba River, three hundred miles from the sea. The banks of the Parnaíba are lined with carnaúba palm, which the explorer Alexander von Humboldt proclaimed the Tree of Providence because every part of it is used: the trunk and thallus for beams and fenceposts, the nuts and palmito for cattle feed, the fronds for straw hats and roof thatch, and the wax coating of the fronds for the manufacture of carbon paper, dry-cell batteries, film, cosmetics, phonograph records, and a hundred and fifty other products. Floriano straddles Piauí's carnaúba and cattle belts, and José Leonias was active in both trades. He bought fronds from the mule trains that came into town and sold them to the factories, where they were stripped of their wax by diesel-powered motors; and he sold jerk beef and leather in his store.

Iraci, the second child, grew to be a striking redhead, and was the first to marry. She fell in love with a tall captain in the Brazilian Air Force band, João Paulo dos Santos, who was playing the trombone in the square one Sunday afternoon. Shortly after their son, Paulo Henrique, was born, dos Santos, on tour with his band, was running after the bus when he fell and struck his head on the pavement. He never recovered completely from the accident. After his release from the hospital he left the Air Force and took a job as the projectionist at Floriano's movie theater. By the time their second child, Ana Goreti, was born, late in 1955, his inexplicable rages had made him impossible to live with, and Iraci returned to her parents. Ana was born five months after Dona Joana's last child; she and Luís Afonso were *irmãos de leite*, "milk brothers," for the two mothers would sometimes take turns nursing each other's child. At one year "Lulu" fell ill, and having been pronounced dead by the doctor, he was laid out on a table in the traditional manner, with a pair of candles at his head and foot. When hot wax from one dropped on his toe, he started crying. "Wait a minute," José Leonias shouted with delighted astonishment. "He isn't dead after all."

In spite of their missing father, Paulo and Ana's childhood seems to have been joyous, and Ana, from whom I have learned most of what I know about the Leonias family, tells me that Floriano is still the main subject of Ana's dreams, the locale of her subconscious life. In her worst nightmare, she is chased by a bull. Paulo, quiet and serious from the beginning, raised a hundred doves in his grandparents' courtyard. Ana played in the street with the neighboring girls games related to prison-ball and ring-around-the-rosy, or jumped from sandpiles that were left in the road during rainy season, or roasted cashew nuts on hot stones till they turned black. On Labor Day, the first of

May, the mayor stuck three hundred cruzeiros on top of a pole greased with cow fat, and all the children would vie for the chance to get them. In another, crueler game, a duck was buried to its head, and the contestants, blindfolded, led away some distance, and spun around, would swat at the air with a plank, but seldom connected with the bird. On January 6, the Feast of the Three Kings, men dressed as cows, vultures, burros, wolves, and other important fauna in the local folklore, pursued by a gleeful throng of children, would go from house to house performing the *forró*, a sort of shuffle with one arm held behind the back and the other across the waist, and a lot of bowing and sweeping. Musicians playing the accordion, the tambourine, and a bamboo fife called the pífano accompanied them.

At least once a day the children went down to the river, carrying baskets of dirty clothes on their heads for the old washerwomen squatting and gossiping at the water's edge. The Parnaíba had a monster called the Cabeça de Cuia, whose head was said to be the size of a large gourd. The creature was attracted to the smoke from the washerwomen's corncob pipes and had already eaten seven washerwomen, all named Maria. One day a man had returned from a fishing trip emptyhanded. His mother was making *chambaril,* the oxfoot stew that is a prized dish in Piauí. In his frustration he picked up a bone and threw it at her. She cast a spell on him: "The river will swallow you unless you eat seven Marias." The children never swam out far because they feared not only the Cabeça de Cuia, but also the whirlpools. The whirlpools swallowed two of Ana's play-mates. Twenty-four hours later their bodies, bloated and partially eaten by piranhas, were found below the point a mile downstream, floating in quiet water. Some afternoons Ana and her friends would just sit and watch the ferryman pulling his boat along the ropes for five hundred yards to the opposite shore, which was in the state of Maranhão. Mesas that seemed blue rose in the distance, and there were two kinds of boats in the water: rafts with steers, mangos, bananas, or carnaúba fronds drifting to Teresina, the capital, two days downriver; or coming back empty, with the men poling laboriously against the current, though this was such hard work that the rafts were more often dismantled at their destination and sold for their lumber. The second kind were the fishermen's dugout canoes, made of *ipê* wood. The best of the day's catch—especially the *surubim,* succulent, brightly striped catfish that got up to three feet—was bought by Dona Joana's brother, João Nepomuceno de Jesus, who had a floating restaurant so famous that the governor usually stopped there when he was in Floriano. On Sunday the whole family often continued from church to Uncle Joe's. The talk at lunch was mostly about the sermon. Padre Pedro, the preacher, was in the habit of strolling in the square, particularly on active evenings like Friday and Saturday, to gather material for his sermons. *"Meus senhores,"* he would report at church the following Sunday. "The other night with my own eyes I saw the daughter of one of the *most respected citizens* of this city shamelessly necking with the son of *another* of our most respected citizens. This is the same young woman who, as I reported last week, was observed BATHING NAKED IN THE RIVER with the same young man. And furthermore"—at this point he would cast an imploring look at the baroque cherubs on the ceiling—"the sons and daughters of our city have BROKEN THE LIGHTS in the square so they can go on petting in the darkness. Is there no shame, I ask you, is there no respect, left in this city of ours?"

Toward suppertime Ana would run past the procession of people carrying water from the river, mostly in ten-gallon kerosene cans; the well in the courtyard spared her that chore. She and her friends would usually stop in front of old Salomita's house to see if they could get a rise out of her. Salomita was an eccentric member of the Castro family, one of Piauí's most prominent. Her cousin, who imported zebu cattle from India, was reputed to be the third-richest man in Brazil. She lived with twenty dogs and an invalid sister in a squalid palm-thatch hut on a large and valuable piece of property. Her dogs were unruly and emaciated. "Hey, Salomita, where are your dogs?" the children would inquire tauntingly. Salomita, who was usually sitting at the door, would then get up, and, shaking a fist, call them "dead sheeps' eyes."

In front of José Leonias' house was a streetlight whose dim, fitful glow, when darkness had fallen, attracted a swarm of crazed moths. Floriano's illumination was mostly provided by kerosene and palm-oil lamps until 1966, when the Boa Esperanca dam, six miles upriver, replaced the fickle Maria Bonita generator as the source of electric power and plunged the region into the age of machinery. The arrival of television, however, was another four years off, and until then the children on the street had to amuse themselves, so they generally met again after supper and played under the streetlight for a few hours. If their racket got out of hand José Leonias would storm out of the house and order them to pipe down. He liked to sit of an evening in his rocker and listen to country music on his big Trans-Globo shortwave radio. Some evenings Ana would stand behind the chair and scratch his head, which was bald. If she stopped he would say, "Oh, terrible child. Leave me in peace." Sometimes he would petrify her with tales of Lôbizonho, the wolfman. It was a good-sized living room, with two sofas and a half-dozen chairs on the cool tile floor. On the walls hung an antique clock with loud chimes, a tinted photograph of José and Dona Joana before their marriage, in an oval frame; and photographs of all the children, including Iraci holding her teacher's diploma. Hooks for hammocks were planted in the walls. Everyone except married couples and guests slept in a hammock. At eight o'clock the children were sent to bed; at ten José Leonias chased his daughters' suitors out of the house with a rolled-up copy of *Manchete,* the Brazilian *Paris Match.* By pretending to be scared of the dark Ana was often allowed to hang her hammock in the living room, and by pretending to be asleep she was able to listen to the adults' conversation. There were often guests from other cities. Circuses would sometimes come to town and because Dona Joana's hotel was near the Campo dos Artistes, the artists would often stay there. One circus played for fifty nights. Ana saw and adored every performance: the clowns, the highwire act, the trapeze artists, the trained bears and lions, the clever dogs, the magician. After ten o'clock there was theater, usually a soap opera adapted from a famous Brazilian novel that took place during the days of slavery. Once—it was perhaps the crowning moment of Ana's childhood—the well-heeled Tiani circus came to town. By some miracle of technology, they converted the stage into an ice rink, and to everyone's amazement, three ballerinas skated in the dripping heat. Occasional bands of gypsies would pass through Floriano, too, pitching their tents in the Campo dos Artistes and offering to read palms. Because of their reputation for lifting things the citizens did not invite them into their houses.

Besides the mule trains, there was a steady flow of people from the parched outback. Half-civilized Indians, naked from the waist up, with long hair and plucked eyebrows, would come from across the river to beg. *Vaqueiros,* the Brazilian cowboys, would blow into town covered with dust and dressed from head to foot in cowhide: boots, chaps, long coats, hats with wide brims bent up or drooping lugubriously over their faces. From his bench under the cashew tree José Leonias would hail even the most disreputable nomad: "Hey there, whoever you are, come down from your horse and have a cup of coffee."

"He was always feeding people who came from the interior to do business in Floriano, people he'd known since childhood who called him *parente,*" one of his children recalled.

"Sometimes there were thirty people at the table," another recalled. "Mother always kept big crocks of rice, beans, sweet manioc, and meat, although she complained of having to feed everyone on the street."

"The spirit of St. Francis was strong in him," corroborated a third. "He was such a good person you had to find the time to talk to him. People made fun of the way he talked. He spoke so deliberately, sitting under the cashew tree, with such a ponderous and respectful patience, that they called him José Paciência. He trusted everyone. 'Go buy this. Bring back the change.' He was good to a fault. People without shame took advantage of him. He kept giving until in the end there was nothing left. In Floriano, they still talk about the fall of José Leonias."

The trouble began in 1950, when one of his wife's brothers-in-law persuaded him, much against his will, to sell his store and buy a truck. Today less than one in every hundred people in Piauí has a car; thirty years ago the fraction was even smaller, and owning a truck was akin to having your own Lear jet. José Leonias knew nothing about trucks—how to keep one running, or even how to drive one. Nevertheless, with a *motorista* on the payroll, he and his brother prospered for several years, hauling goods back and forth from Recife, six hundred miles away. But one day in 1957 the truck exploded, and that finished him. There was still the hotel, and Dona Joana started a bakery, making bread and cakes in a brick oven in the courtyard. But his fortunes never recovered from that involvement with the truck, and in his last years he was obliged to work as the timekeeper in a construction yard. By 1960 there was nothing to keep José Leonias' children or grandchildren in Floriano. When he died at sixty-three of a heart attack at two o'clock after lunch on March 14, 1974, only his wife and their son Mario, a surveyor in Teresina, were still in Piauí. Many of them had moved to the country's new capital, Brasília, where I became acquainted with Ana and her family. Francisco and Ana last visited Floriano in 1976. "The son and granddaughter of José

10

Leonias arrived today in a car with license plates
CAPITAL OF THE REPUBLIC," the local paper a...
and the following day it reported that Francisco Leonias had
been seen "drinking beer on Monday afternoon," a noteworthy
fact because few citizens of Piauí could afford to keep drinking
past the weekend. The house on the corner of Ruas Floriano
Peixoto and Padre Uchôa is empty and deteriorating from
neglect. José Leonias left no will, and for his wife to sell it, she
would need the signatures of her eleven remaining children and
her twenty-eight grandchildren. Not all of them want it sold,
because it is their last tie with their homeland.

———————

Few expressions are more overworked than the term "a land
of contrasts." I know a half-dozen books about the most
different countries, each of whose subtitles is "land of contrasts." But in Brazil the disparities—between the South and
the North, the coast and the interior, the rich and the poor—are
so prominent that the term is transcendently apt. Perhaps it is
because the country is simultaneously at so many stages of
cultural evolution, from the aboriginal hunter-gatherer to the
fully Western and up-to-the-minute member of the Pepsi
generation. One of the contrasts was brought home on our last
trip to Brazil, when the bill for a twin bed in Rio de Janeiro
came to more than the annual per capita income in Piauí for
1968. In that year, the last for which I was able to get statistics,
the annual per capita income was sixty dollars. Most of the
people made even less than that, because the figure was
averaged with a few incomes that were extremely substantial.
"The trouble with per capita income," a third-world economist
explained, "is that nobody has it." And in a place like Piauí,

11

most of whose population is only marginally involved in the money economy, the per capita concept has even less meaning. From the air, flying out of one of the saturated cities on the coast, the second contrast soon became apparent: 80 percent of the population lives within two hundred miles of the Atlantic; the rest of Brazil is virtually empty. Amazonia, which takes up 57 percent of the country's 3,284,000 square miles, would have boasted in 1970 an average of 2.7 people per square mile, had they suddenly been turned out of the handful of population centers. It is the world's greatest demographic void, emptier than any of the deserts. In a jet plane several hours are required to fly over its unbroken canopy, where, in the evocative description of Euclides da Cunha, "the last chapter of Genesis is being enacted." In 1960 Piauí, Maranhâo, and ten other states in the Federation of Brazil were still technically uninhabited. (For an area to qualify as uninhabited, most human geographers require an average density of at least five people per square mile.) For a country its size, Brazil's population is remarkably small. It did not pass the fifty million mark until 1950, and now stands—thanks to one of the world's most vigorous growth curves—at about one hundred and fifteen; but this is only somewhat more than twice the population of the United Kingdom on thirty-five times the area. (But it must be pointed out, in all fairness, that this is more than all the rest of the people in South America put together.) Though parts of it were reached four hundred and fifty years ago, much of northern Brazil is still wilderness or rowdy frontier. Maps of the country, sparsely dotted with symbols of human occupation and even more sparsely meshed with connective arteries, adorn the walls of homes, bars, stores, and offices throughout the region. Why, the North American visitor wonders, is this great country, so like ours, still in a state of innocence? Brazilians like the sociologist Viana Moog are equally puzzled. "How was it possible," he asked in the 1950s, "for the United States, a country smaller in its contiguous continental area, to achieve the almost miraculous progress that it has, whereas Brazil, whose history antedates that of the United States by more than a century, still appears only the uncertain land of the future?" Many of the most likely explanations were covered in his book *Bandeirantes and Pioneers*. In the first place, the characters of the two settlements were different: in North America it was spiritual, practical, and constructive; in South America it was predatory, extractive, and only secondarily religious. The exploration of Brazil began in earnest a century after it was sighted, on April 22, 1500. Setting forth from a few already thriving colonial outposts, the Portuguese *bandeirantes*, or "flagbearers," were the Brazilian counterparts of the *conquistadores*. "Their eyes dilated by greed," they seldom settled in the territories they crossed. They came without families in the hope of finding fabulous wealth and returning to Portugal as soon as possible. Abducting or massacring the local population, and introducing it to smallpox, malaria, tuberculosis, measles, the cold virus, and other diseases to which it had no resistance, they contributed more to the depopulation than to the peopling of Brazil. The few with higher motives felt themselves on a divine mission, and were possessed by an almost Islamic otherworldliness. Their first order of business, after deciding to inhabit a place, was to erect the most splendid church imaginable, and most of their energies over the next few decades were devoted to that end. The North American pioneers, on the other hand, came with their families to settle permanently in the New World. Taking the land inch by inch, they planted towns and cities. For them the great virtues were thrift, hard work and the productive utilization of time—while for the Catholic *bandeirantes* they were theological.

Another important factor was that Brazil was a colony—in other words, its own interests were ignored—until 1822. It existed solely to enrich Portugal, at first through the cutting of brazilwood, later through the cultivation of sugarcane. European civilization did not reach its shore until its first emperor, Dom Pedro, an admirer of Napoleon, brought it from France. Portugal itself could hardly be offered as a model of progress or prosperity. Reactionary governments in both Spain and Portugal had tried to keep the status of their colonies unchanged, and the parent countries themselves had been left behind by the rest of Europe. It was partly due to the Church, whose disapproval of science and technology prevented Spain and Portugal from entering the twentieth century until only a few years ago. "Today," as a Brazilian novelist observed, "our matrix, Portugal, is worse off than we are." In comparison, by the early nineteenth century America was already beginning to realize its manifest destiny, and England was in the throes of industrial revolution. The lack of democracy and personal freedom in Brazil, after a decade and a half of military rule, was until recently another frequent if never attributable explanation for the country's failure to develop more rapidly. "People aren't productive unless they're happy," a dentist told me. This argument, however, has more truth with respect to the whole course of Brazilian history than to the last fifteen years, which have been materially, at least, a period of tremendous advancement.

After the first rush to Brazil in the sixteenth century, the flow of immigrants dwindled almost to nothing, which explains, along with a high tropical death rate, the country's relatively minute population. Those who came "carried intermarriage to extremes never known previously," as Moog writes. Miscegenation with largely demoralized and passive slaves and Indians blurred the racial divisions that have darkened the histories of many other countries; but at the same time it undoubtedly contributed to Brazil's inability to keep up with the pace of European development. About 1820, the Germans started coming, and the country was infused with new blood. The largest infusion, four million foreigners—not only Germans, but Italians, Japanese, Spanish, and Dutch—came during the fifty years before World War II; after the war the enormous number of displaced people forced Brazil to tighten its immigration policies. Highly disciplined and motivated, the Germans quickly outcompeted the natives and brought the standard of living in southern Brazil up to that of the motherland. Their offspring hold key positions in industry and government: the last president, Ernesto Geisel, was the son of immigrants, while the minister of finance until his dismissal in early 1980, was the fiercely competent Karlos Rischbieter. The Germans tend to keep to themselves and to marry their own kind, seldom succumbing to the attractions of a raven-haired Lusitanian, and even more rarely to those of a beautiful *mulata*. Many have thinly disguised contempt for the other ethnic groups, laying the general backwardness of Latin America on what one described as "the Iberian curse," and the disparity between the North and South of Brazil on, to use Moog's wording, "the congenital superiority of the blond, blue-eyed dolichocephalic type over the rest of humanity."

In addition to whatever human shortcomings there may have been, the geographical barriers to conquering Brazil were already formidable enough. While most of North America is eminently suitable for human occupation, most of South America is either comparable to, say the rocky sections of Colorado, or else thick jungle. In Brazil the rivers do not lead to the sources of natural wealth, and, during the period of its settlement, access to the interior was blocked by rapids, hostile Indians, and the rugged mountains that line most of the coast. In the North the great enemy of progress was the climate: the staggering heat of the Northeast, which geologists now consider a severed piece of the great dry zone in southwestern Africa; the stifling humidity of the Amazon. In both regions the people seem incapable of long-range ambition. Even Germans become

15

sluggish. Of all the possible explanations for why civilization is more retarded in the tropics, the simplest one, climate, is probably the most important. Where winter never comes there is no need to plan ahead, to become a serious farmer (the first step toward civilization), or to produce heat in any quantity (the first step toward industrialization). Not that it is an easy place to live: the insects, the riot of debilitating microorganisms, and the widespread shortage of protein include it with the most forbidding environments. Another factor, surprising in the lush forests of the Amazon, is the soil's extreme poverty. Betty Meggers, a cultural ecologist at the Smithsonian Institution, concludes in her study, *Amazonia: Counterfeit Paradise,* that most of the region is only capable of supporting small-scale, shifting agriculture. This is also true of the Northeast and the Central Plateau, where centuries of wind and rain have swept away the soil and humus, leaving only sunbaked hardpan. Geographers Janet Henshall and Richard Momsen write, "the land and its resources never seem to have quite lived up to the original promise they were thought to hold, resulting in a dispersal of effort, a picking over of opportunities and the eventual neglect or abandonment of once-enticing possibilities."

By the middle of this century it was clear that if Brazil—the whole country, and not just the South—was ever going to become more than "a land of promise," something dramatic would have to be done to rectify the imbalance of its settlement and development patterns. People would somehow have to be coaxed from the littoral, the blank interior filled, and the Northeast, whose thirty million poor form the greatest concentration of misery in Latin America, would somehow have to be made to prosper. Some bold gesture, like relocating the capital, was indicated. This was not a new idea. It had been gestating in the national consciousness, in fact, for nearly two hundred years. In 1761 the Marquis of Pombal, a Lusitanian nobleman, had lobbied for the construction of a city in the backlands of Pernambuco that would serve not only as the capital of the colony, but as the seat of the Portuguese throne. Far from the sea, it would be safe from external menace, while halfway between the important trade routes to Africa and the East Indies. In 1808, after the invasion of Portugal by Napoleon, the court of Queen Donna Maria I was hastily transported to Brazil, but it reconvened in Rio de Janeiro, and not in Pernambuco. Sixteen years before Tiradentes, or "Tooth-puller," the leader of a popular uprising and Brazil's first national hero, had tried to get the capital moved from Rio to Sao João del Rei in the mountains of Minas Gerais. The rebellion was put down, but the idea did not die. In 1810 Veloso de Oliveira, chancellor of the Court of Donna Maria and Dom João VI, Prince of Brazil, urged "that the court not be located at any seaport, especially if it be great and well-suited for commerce, but in a healthy, agreeable spot from the turmoil of indiscriminately accumulated people." Three years later, José Hipólito de Costa Furtado de Mendonça wrote in an editorial for the *Correio Brasiliense,* a paper he had started in London five years earlier:

> Rio de Janeiro possesses not one of the qualities required for the city that is destined to be the capital of the Empire of Brazil, and if the courtiers who came here from Lisbon had enough patriotism and gratitude for the country that received them at the time of their trouble, then they would make a generous sacrifice of the amenities and such luxury as they enjoy in Rio and would go and establish themselves in a region of the interior central and immediate to the headwaters of the great rivers, and there erect a new city, begin to open up roads that would lead to every seaport, remove the natural obstacles from the navigable rivers and thus lay the foundations of the most extensive, well-linked, -protected, and powerful empire that could possibly exist

Alex Shoumatoff

on the surface of the earth, given the actual condition of the countries that populate it. This central point is to be found at the headwaters of the famous Rio São Francisco. In its vicinity are the fountainheads of copious rivers that lead to the north and the south, to the northeast and the southwest, vast prairies for the raising of cattle, rock in abundance for every sort of building, lumber for every necessity, the richest mines for every type of metal—a situation that could be compared with the description we have of Paradise on earth.

On October 9, 1821, the eve of Brazil's independence, José Bonifacio da Andrade de Silva sent among his instructions from the Provisional Government of São Paulo to the deputies at the court of Lisbon (with Napoleon no longer a threat, the royal family had gone back to Portugal) the following recommendation: "It would seem to be a very good step if a city were built in the center of the interior of Brazil, at a latitude of more or less fifteen degrees, as the seat of the Court of the Regency, and that roads to the different provinces and ports be opened, both to facilitate the speedy communication of orders and to encourage domestic trade within the empire." A year later, Brazil seceded. The Portuguese king, João VI, wasn't pleased, but there was little he could do about it. The new, self-proclaimed emperor, Dom Pedro, was his son, the prince regent, and had the unequivocal backing of everyone in the country. In a postscript to the constitution for the new empire that was drafted in Lisbon, mention of the word Brasília first appears: "In the center of Brazil, among the springs at the joint source of the Paraguay and the Amazon, to found the capital of the realm, with the denomination of Brasília or some other."

But the resolution languished on paper and Rio de Janeiro, far from the geographical heart of the country, remained the capital. The idea of Brasília, however, retained a utopian

18

fascination for men like Francisco Adolfo de Varnhagen, the future Viscount of Pôrto Seguro, who in 1883, returning from an expedition to the Central Plateau, enthusiastically proposed as the ideal site "the triangle between Lakes Formosa, Feia, and Mestre d'Armes," where the Amazon, Prata, and São Francisco rivers have their beginning. At one thousand meters, the climate is superb, he argued, and the site equidistant from the cities of Rio to the south, Bahia to the northeast, Oeiras to the northeast, Cuiabá to the west, and Curitiba to the southwest. This was, it would turn out, the right general area. But even more prescient was the vision that came to the mystic, Father Giuseppe Bosco, in Turin, Italy, on the night of August 30, 1883. Several of Father Bosco's prophetic dreams had already come true. That night's dream was about the grandiose future of South America. His congregation listened intently as he related a few days later how he had been carried away by angels. "My eyes acquired a marvelous acuity and I saw unfolding before me various stupendous regions—swamps, mountains, plains, the Amazon jungle with its intricate and enormous rivers." He visited the huts of Indians and, terrified, watched a human sacrifice in which two Salesian missionaries were beaten to death with clubs—the precise fate that fathers Pedro Sacilloti and João Fuchs would meet in 1934 at the hands of the Xavantes. But that wasn't all. "Between the fifteenth and twentieth parallels," he continued, "beginning at a point where a lake had formed, there was a fairly wide and extensive depression. And a voice kept telling me repeatedly, 'When the mines hidden in the heart of these mountains are tapped, a great civilization will appear here, the Promised Land, flowing with milk and honey. It will be an inconceivable richness. And this will happen in the third generation." Father Bosco died five years later and was canonized not for his visions, but for his contributions as an educator, by Pius the Eleventh. The first masonry structure that went up in Brasília was his shrine, a small, steep-sided pyramid that overlooks the city from the scrubby hillside across the lake. Though a shantytown had grown up half a mile away, when I visited it twenty years later, and people there could have used the cruzeiro notes that had been stuffed into the tin can before his statue, the offerings were intact. In a nearby tree a metallic green hummingbird was gushing forth with metallic pings whose volume was startling.

In 1891 the government, no longer an empire and now a republic, affirmed its belief in Brasília, decreeing, in the third article of the new constitution, that an area of 5,500 square miles be set aside in the Central Plateau for the site of the future Federal District. The following year a twenty-two-man commission, headed by Luís Cruls, president of the National Observatory, and including a botanist, a geologist, an engineer, a surveyor, a doctor, a pharmacist, and a photographer, set out for the interior. Leaving Rio on the ninth of June, they went by train to the end of the line at Uberaba, and proceeded by horse to Pirenópolis, where they split into two groups. Under trying conditions they managed to complete the first detailed scientific study of the region, collecting plants, minerals, and soil samples, measuring the flow of sixteen rivers and the magnetic declination at five points, and surveying an area enclosed by two degrees of longitude and two of latitude. Cruls was as taken with the region as Varnhagen had been. The European immigrant, he predicted, would encounter a climate analogous with the most salubrious in the temperate zones, and would have no trouble adapting. "Is it not then fitting," he asked, "to try to give that immense region the life that it lacks?" But again the idea glowed with brief brilliance and then, like a meteor, slipped from view. Someone in the Congress proposed that the city be constructed without onus to the government, that any private company agreeing to undertake the project be allowed to control the services of the city—light, water, sewage, transport, and the like—for ninety years. But there were no takers. Sporadic political gestures kept the idea alive. In 1922 President Epitácio Pessôa ordered that "the necessary steps be taken to place, at the most appropriate spot, the cornerstone of the future city, that will be the Capital of the Union." Accordingly a delegation was despatched to the interior and on September 7 erected a small obelisk outside the sleepy town of Planaltina, where it still stands, guarded by a man in a khaki uniform. Other speeches and decrees were made in 1934, 1937, and 1946, when the president of the Republic was given sixty days to appoint "a committee of technical engineers of recognized standing to proceed with the study of the location of the new capital." In swift compliance with the edict a commission under General Poli Coelho headed for the interior and not only expanded the area surveyed by the Cruls Commission to 29,750 square miles, but also discovered another promising site in Minas Gerais. The presence of a new candidate plunged the Congress into five years of debate, at the end of which the whole matter reverted to square one, namely, where the new capital ought to be. It fell on Getúlio Vargas, who had been president on and off for thirty years, to appoint a final, definitive commission. An American firm that specialized in aerial photographs, Donald Belcher and Associates of Ithaca, New York, was retained to provide basic maps, transparencies, scale models, core samples, and detailed evaluations of five sites of 19,320 square miles each chosen by the commission. The Belcher Report, as it became known, was delivered at the end of February 1955. It is an epic and all but forgotten work of which few copies exist in Brasília. Only with great reluctance did a city planner in the annex of the governor's palace finally unlock his cabinet and let me borrow his well-thumbed photocopy. From the beginning, Belcher and Associates seem to have been aware of the importance of what they had been asked to do. Almost all the great cities of the world, the report pointed out, have had an insignificant, almost accidental beginning, becoming more important than other settlements because they were near natural paths of commerce, sources of raw materials, or because they were relatively impregnable. Most of them have grown organically along large bays, at the mouths of rivers with good access to the interior, at strategic military points, and in other privileged spots, and their success—the augmentation of their population and prestige— has always been dependent on geographical factors, whether consciously selected or not. But there is another kind of city that comes into being as the result of a deliberate choice. The classic example is St. Petersburg: Peter the Great wanted "a window on the West," and thirty thousand peasants died in the marshes of the Neva to give it to him. A surprising number of other cities have been catapulted into being over the centuries, mostly to serve as seats of government. Beginning in ancient Egypt there were Memphis and Thebes, and the fantastic city of Akhetaton, which Pharaoh Amenhotep IV had built to oppose the reaction- ary clergy of the god Amon, who were pontificating in Thebes, the existing capital. In China, there was Peking. Japan, starting in the twelfth century, was curiously endowed with two capitals: Kyoto was the traditional residence of the mikado, while Kamakura and later Yedo were administrative centers of the shogun, the military dictator. Not to mention Madrid, Washing- ton, Ottawa, Pretoria, Ankara, Canberra, and New Delhi.

Brasília would belong to this tradition. Like St. Petersburg it was far from any existing population or agricultural centers. What would ensure its success was that it would be the center of government; roads, people, and commerce would follow. As with St. Petersburg, its creation would serve to pull together a vast and largely backward country, but instead of looking to the West, to countries further down the road of progress, Brazil would turn into itself, in a new surge of national pride and self- discovery, to its own virgin heartland. To Belcher and Associ- ates Brasília offered an unprecedented chance to build a city in equilibrium with its surroundings. The technical aspects of city planning were more advanced than they had ever been, the state of the art had become so intricate and comprehensive in recent years that it was virtually a new discipline; and the great cities had been around long enough for their flaws, the initial errors of judgment and the outright oversights, to be plainly visible to those who understood what they were looking for. To the Brazilians involved in the project it became steadily clearer that the history of their country would soon be divided into two parts: Before Brasília, and After. They were aware of doing three things: integrating the country, "interiorizing" progress, and providing a quiet, inspiring setting in which national decisions could be made. But few yet realized that the project had an even larger implication.

By the mid-twentieth century the human population had grown so, and society had gotten so complex that the creation of new cities was no longer a spontaneous process. Cities from now on would be "rationally planned" usurpations of habitat. Most of the earth's prime habitat had already been spoken for, but mankind had lately acquired the technology to establish sizable installations—even full-scale metropolises—on second- and even third-rate terrain. And the first of these new cities in out-of-the-way places would be Brasília. Instead of being a product of regional growth, it would create a region.

The five sites, colored green, red, blue, yellow, and brown, were all in the same gently undulating terrain, covered with savanna grasses and the small, warped trees characteristic of the region. None of them was clearly superior to the others in every respect, Belcher and Associates realized as they held them up to a long list of criteria. There must be no scarps, gorges, morasses, or mountain ranges in the vicinity to impede the expansion of the city; but there should be a few natural accidents that could be exploited for recreational ends. The topography should offer some variety to avoid monotony, but no slope could be more than eight degrees. Strong breezes should play on the site to keep it free of haze. The soil should be solid enough for road-building, deep and rich enough to support vegetation, yet well-drained and friable for sewage disposal by gravity; the report went on for nearly two hundred pages just about the soil factors. At the same time the bedrock had to be near enough the surface for the foundations of large buildings to sit firmly, without being *so* near that space for subterranean utility lines would have to be blasted. You didn't want the problems of cities like Amsterdam, Mexico City, Bangkok, Istanbul, Boston, and Chicago, which had been built on soft, humid subsoils and deep bedrock. Techniques for preventing building regression had been around since 1930, but they raised the cost of construction by 30 percent. Nor did you want a repetition of what had happened in Amsterdam, Washington, and Cairo, which were far from sources of raw materials for building. Having them more than eighteen miles away quintupled the price of sand, rock, and fill. Nearby, too, should be a source of water; if higher than the site of the city, all the better. There should be enough water for five hundred thousand people, not to mention irrigation, the watering of parks, the filling of pools, and the spouting of such fountains as a well-appointed capital would inevitably require. Dams would almost certainly be installed, and to that end calcareous substrates, too porous to be capable of water retention, were to be shunned; any site with honeycomb limestone, caverns, sinkholes, or subterranean rivers in the neighborhood would have to be ruled out immediately. So were those with any danger of flooding, and those where the logistics of tying in with the existing highway and railroad networks were forbidding.

The prettiest site, Blue, was in Minas Gerais, with streams and buriti palms; but the stream volume was inadequate and there were karst formations nearby. Yellow, in the state of Goiás, didn't have good water, either, and further west, where Green was, the country got too rough. The trouble with Red, in the broadest valley of the region, was that it had too many owners to be expropriated easily. Only Brown, at 15°30′ latitude, had no serious drawbacks. Its physiognomy—a gently sloping triangular dome defined by three rivers: Corrego Fundo, Riberão Bananal, and Rio Paranoá, was entirely different from that of the other four; at elevations ranging from thirty-two hundred to thirty-nine hundred feet, it was also the highest of the candidates. The views were superb, the drainage good, and there was the requisite flatness for large buildings and an airport. In short, the report concluded unemotionally, "this site is suitable for a large city." Years later, the project's field manager admitted that they may have slanted the findings slightly because they were so favorably impressed with Brown. But there was absolutely no truth, he said, to the rumor one still occasionally hears in Brasília that Brown was chosen because the land belonged to "someone high up."

As soon as the report was delivered, Marshal José Pessôa, head of the commission, bushwhacked to Brown by jeep; it was thirty-five miles southeast of Planaltina, where the cornerstone had been laid in 1922. Pessôa was delighted with the site. As far as he was concerned, the location of the new capital was settled. All that was needed now was a president who would stop hemming and hawing and bring the city to life. For centuries it had been waiting for birth, but the country, still huddled on the Atlantic and looking to Europe, had not been ready. Now, perhaps, Brasília was an idea whose time had come. It was true that there was still not even a paved road from Rio to Belo Horizonte, the capital of Minas Gerais, four hundred and fifty miles southeast of Brown, from which most of the materials and the equipment would have to come. But with planes, with the help of modern air transport, the city could be started, and then the roadbuilders would have somewhere to build the road to. Without a concrete destination, it was unlikely that the road-builders would even want to begin. So that problem was not insurmountable. Nor were any of the others, really. Brazil in 1955 was at that economic and psychological point that is sometimes called "emergent." A challenge like this was just what she needed; it was high time for the people to rise up and assert themselves over the land. All that was needed was a leader. The suicide of Getúlio Vargas on September 24, 1954, with the Belcher Report five months from completion, suddenly altered the entire political picture in Brazil. It looked as if a coalition of three parties—the PSD, the PTB, and the PR—would nominate as their candidate for the 1955 elections the dynamic young governor of Minas Gerais, Juscelino Kubitschek.

Juscelino—he was so straightforward and accessible that everyone knew him by his first name—was the sort of leader that a country is lucky to get once in a century. Like Teddy Roosevelt and J.F.K., he had the gift of making you want to do something just because he was involved in it, and there was nothing small or invidious about him. He had grown up in circumstances not unlike those of the Leonias family in Diamantina, a lost city in the hinterland of Minas Gerais noted for its steep cobbled streets, its inspired Baroque churches, its diamond mines, its prominent role in the Tiradentes rebellion, and Chica da Silva, a stunning *mulata* slave who eventually became a queen of Brazil. Juscelino's grandfather had migrated from the village of Tresbon, Bohemia, late in the previous century. The word kubitschek means "little barrel." The people of Diamantina called him Joe the German, although he was in fact a Czech. He was an avid reader; when he wasn't working as a carpenter he was usually stretched out in his hammock with a book. He died from burns received when his house caught fire and he ran inside to rescue his library. His daughter Julia married a poet named João César de Oliveira, who was like the charming grasshopper in La Fontaine. He went from town to town, selling things and telling stories in the tradition of the medieval troubadours of Europe. The itinerant peddlers were the newspapers of the day. Oliveira died of tuberculosis at the age of thirty-two, succumbing after an all-night serenade. From his father, Juscelino got his "Bohemian" (which in Brazil means freewheeling and unconventional) side; from his strong-willed mother, the actual Bohemian, widowed at twenty-nine with two children, his enormous self-discipline and capacity for work. Julia was ambitious for her son. "Fear God and never people like yourself," she would frequently tell him. In Brazil the maternal and paternal last names carry equal weight. Juscelino took his mother's name, as many Brazilians do. She called him "Nono" to distinguish him from his sister, Nana. At ten Nono was devouring Voltaire, Racine, Molière, Balzac, Zola, and Jules Verne. Every spare cruzeiro was spent to order books from Rio. At fifteen he entered a school for telegraphists in Belo Horizonte; Julia had pawned her father's wedding ring to pay the tuition. Hammering out telegrams by night, Juscelino studied medicine. His father's and grandfather's early deaths and the lack of medical facilities in Diamantina had convinced him that a contribution could be made in that field. So conscientiously did he apply himself to his studies that in a few years he had absorbed what there was to learn in Belo Horizonte, and proceeded to Paris, where he apprenticed with a famous surgeon; and there, exploring the galleries and the libraries, he formed a lasting admiration for the civilization of France. Returning to Belo Horizonte, he set up surgical practice as a kidney specialist and soon prospered. But in 1932 an insurrection called the Constitutionalist Revolution broke out in São Paulo. Its purpose was to overthrow the two-year-old government of Getúlio Vargas, which had itself been installed by a new revolution, and to get a new constitution that would clean up the voting system. This conflict pitted the citizens of Minas Gerais against those of São Paulo, and Juscelino, drafted into the Military Police, went to the front to take charge of a field hospital. While operating on the wounded, he became aware for the first time of his natural administrative capacities, and working sometimes twenty hours a day, he cleaned up the chaotic mess in which he had found the hospital. Young Kubitschek's drive and organizational talent impressed his superiors, especially Benedito Valadares, who, after the conclusion of the hostilities, was appointed governor of Minas Gerais. Valadares asked Juscelino to join his staff.

Juscelino accepted but soon grew bored and returned to his practice. But he had acquired a taste for politics, and having been exposed to even larger social problems, he could no longer look at his profession in the same way. What good was his medicine, how could public health programs reach the majority of Brazilians, until there were better roads, communications, and the general level of education was dramatically raised? In 1939 Valadares asked him to be mayor of Belo Horizonte. He took the job and in six years completely remodeled the city, tearing up the cobbled streets and paving them with asphalt, installing water, sewage, and electric lines. Because of the wartime shortage of gasoline, the work was done with ten thousand wagons drawn by burros. In a district called Pampulha he commissioned an innovative young architect named Oscar Niemeyer to design residential development, with a casino, a yacht club, and a chapel built mostly of glass, overlooking an artificial lake. There began a most fruitful partnership. Though neither of them yet knew it, Belo Horizonte was a dry run, a testing ground for energies and abilities that would be called upon a decade later for a far greater project. As mayor, Juscelino proved himself a dynamo, a wild, exuberant creator of landscapes on an almost empty canvas. His success there led to the governorship of Minas Gerais and finally, in 1955, to the presidential nomination. As a candidate, Kubitschek gave no sign that he had even heard of the Belcher Report or given any thought to the obscure clause in the 1891 constitution that called for a new capital to be built on the Planalto Central. It was a time of political uncertainty that had led to the removal from office of João Café Filho, the vice-president who had taken over after the death of Vargas, and his replacement by Carlos Luz, president of the Chamber of Deputies, and later by Nereú Ramos, president of the Senate. Wisely, Juscelino based his campaign on a return to "law and order," on rigorous compliance with the constitution. On April 4, speaking in the main square of Jataí, a small, remote city in Goiás, he opened the floor to questions, as he had learned to do during his gubernatorial campaign. Goiás was the state that encompassed Brown. Jataí means "You're already here." A man near the bandstand named Antonio Carvalho Soares, nicknamed Toniquinho, raised his hand and asked, "You say that if elected you'll stick to the constitution. Does that mean, then, that you plan to put into practice the directive that orders that the federal capital be moved to the Planalto Central?" Juscelino was momentarily at a loss. He had already announced his platform, and none of its thirty planks made any reference to the matter. But he gave the only answer he saw possible. "I've just promised that I would comply, in full, with the constitution, and I see no reason why this directive should be ignored. If elected I will build the new capital and see that the seat of government is moved." This affirmation provoked wild applause. For a long time the people of Goiás had been cherishing the dream of Brasília, and for the first time they had heard a candidate for the presidency of the Republic solemnly pledge to give it life.

From this almost offhanded beginning, Kubitschek's support of Brasília was a point of honor. But the more he thought about it, as the view from his train window reminded him of the emptiness and the misery of much of Brazil, the more he realized that the relocation of the capital could serve as a vehicle for the Brazilian people to take possession of their vast territory

29

and to break out of the poverty in which 60 percent of them lived. "During our entire history, from the Discovery to my regime," Juscelino wrote in his delightfully informal memoir, *Why I Built Brasília,* "we lived, to use the observation of our first historian, Friar Vincent of Salvador, 'scratching the sand of the beach, like crabs.'" The country's economy was "marasmic." Goods took months to reach the interior, as the child who had waited impatiently for books from Rio well knew. In 1955 the per capita income in Brazil was $228, less than half that in many other Latin American countries: Argentina had $697; Chile, $539; Colombia, $374; Costa Rica, $507; Cuba, $613; Mexico, $372; Panama, $468; Uruguay, $679; Venezuela, $921. Juscelino proposed a crash program, "Fifty years in five," as his infectious campaign slogan promised. Five years was all he had, because the constitution forbade a president to serve consecutive terms. In fact, after the project finally cleared the Congress, only three years and ten months were left in which to build the city. From the beginning time was always the greatest problem. One sentence in the Belcher Report bothered Juscelino: "the planning body has recognized, in the course of its study, that the building of the city should proceed *in stages."* Given the nature of Brazilian politics, this was impossible. "It is an ancient tradition in Brazil," he explained, "that no administration has ever brought to a successful conclusion any work initiated by its antecedent." Juscelino would have to present his successors with a whole city, a fait accompli. The short time for construction was one of the chief objections in the Congress. Others felt that Brasília was inopportune; still too soon. Others questioned whether it was really necessary, whether the money needed for its construction might not better be applied to improving conditions in the Northeast, opening up the Amazon, cleaning up the vast *favelas,* or shantytowns, in Rio, São Paulo, Salvador, Recife, and every other city; or to dozens of other problems that were (and still are) pressing in Brazil.

30

Juscelino was well aware of these problems, and the way to begin dealing with them, he urged, was to shift the country's center of gravity by moving the capital. Although a small opposition would keep trying, right up to the inauguration, to paralyze the project, he finally won the begrudging support of the Congress and immediately created two agencies: NOVACAP, in charge of building the new capital and transferring the government to it; and the Banco Regional, empowered to float bond issues and allocate funds. A close friend, now the Brasília bureau chief of *O Globo,* the country's most powerful newspaper, explained how Juscelino put together the money for the city: "You remember how Ulysses Grant got the railroad built from the Atlantic to the Pacific? When he opened it, the coolies who had done the work came to him and complained, 'Our pockets are full of phony money.' Puffing on a cigar, Grant replied, 'The money may be phony, but the railroad is real.' Well, it was the same with Juscelino. The project was very costly. The first brick came in Air Force planes. To pay for it, he inflated the currency. He had to. People said, 'This is an *absurdo.*' He said, 'Yes, this is an *absurdo,* but the capital is here.' It was the only way to do it. If it had been all meticulously planned and budgeted it still wouldn't be finished.".

When José Pessôa, head of the Location Commission, agreed with the Belcher Report that the capital should be built in stages, he was eased out of the project. Juscelino knew that the people who built the city would have to be unwilling to accept half measures. There was at least one man of vision on whom he could already count. Driving around Rio with Oscar Niemeyer one afternoon in the beginning of 1956, soon after he had become president, he asked, "How would you like to be my Michelangelo?" Hearing the particulars, Oscar dropped everything. Juscelino virtually gave him carte blanche. Few architects have a whole city handed them. This was the opportunity of a lifetime, and Oscar jumped at it. In a few weeks he had closed his Copacabana studio and flown to Brasília, where he would spend most of the next six years living in a single-room shack papered with sketches of monumental buildings. Although he could have named his salary, he would take only a modest governmental retainer of three hundred dollars a month. By the inauguration he had lost nineteen pounds from his already lean frame.

Oscar was perhaps the brightest of Le Corbusier's Latin American disciples. They had worked together in 1936 on the iconoclastic new Ministry of Education in Rio. Le Corbusier was, of course, the father of the modern glass box. Dispensing with brick, stone, and mortar, eliminating moldings and every other form of ornamentation that put in relief and therefore emphasized the existence of outer walls, he hung shimmering sheets of glass from steel frames. "Architecture," he wrote, "is the masterly, correct, and magnificent play of masses brought together in light." His buildings stood pure and singular in the confusion of nature. He took his modernism to radical extremes. His 1925 Voisin Plan had called for the wholesale razing of Paris and its replacement with a grid of independent towers separated by green spaces and linked by freeways. Fortunately it was never carried out. A decade later, in the course of six public lectures, he outlined his solution to the already entrenched congestion of Rio: there would be a second city of unprecedented form, raised on pilings a hundred and twenty feet above the existing one, and a hundred and eighty feet higher than that, an eighty-foot-wide freeway linking the hilltops and the various *bairros* that had grown haphazardly on the margins of the bay. This wasn't done either, but Oscar and the other Brazilian architects were enthralled by the cataclysmic simplicity of Le Corbusier's ideas. Most of the young intellectuals in Latin America at that time were eager to break with the past and take a long leap forward, and in the coming decades the influence of Le Corbusier, whose glass buildings incarnated their yearnings, would dominate the skylines of São Paulo, Bogotá, Caracas, Mexico City, and finally Brasília.

———————

Today, with his city twenty years old and thriving, Niemeyer is the dean of Brazilian architecture. His Copacabana studio—the same one he had when Juscelino summoned him—is in a pink building locally referred to as the Mae West because of two bulges of bay windows that run up its curved front. In the first room, when I dropped in, young men and women were bent over drafting tables. Oscar was through two more doors. He was short, intense, dark-complexioned, a man who neither looked nor acted like a seventy-three-year-old. He had joined the Communist Party in 1945 and still considered himself a rebel. He gave me a slim volume called *Form in Architecture,* which he had written, dedicating it with *um abraço.* It was part of a series of writings by leftist Brazilian intellectuals that his own publishing concern was printing. "I've never forgotten—I was eight years old—hearing my grandfather say to the servant girl, 'Take that scarf from your head. A negro doesn't wear such things.' Then, it was life itself that showed its miseries: the boss oppressing the servant, the poorer friend passed over, the destitution that afflicts our Brazilian brothers, and the ignorant bourgeoisie that oppresses them or shows itself paternalistic or irresponsible. There could be no doubt which position to take in a country where 70 percent of the population suffer, exploited and persecuted."

His art, like Le Corbusier's, had an explicit egalitarian aim. "I remember one of the many times," he began, "when I was hauled up before the Political Police. They asked me what we were trying to do. I said, 'Change society.' Most architects are very shut up in their profession. They don't want to be involved, they don't see the cultural implications of what they're doing. But the best architecture is a social architecture that desires to see basic reform. For me it all began in Pampulha in the forties, with the wonderful chance that Juscelino gave me. In those days, cold, rigid, monotonous functionalism predominated. We wanted to break with stagnant tradition, to inject a little fantasy." A few months after this interview, I made a pilgrimage to Pampulha. Belo Horizonte had swarmed over Juscelino's thirty-year-old improvements and become a noisy, hot, appallingly coagulated city again; but Pampulha was a lush, gracious oasis, a Brazilian Coral Gables tastefully withdrawn from the din. The Casino, since the outlawing of gambling in 1947, had become a small museum of modern art whose driveway was overgrown with weeds and whose visitors' book had that day been signed by only three people. The attendant led us up a ramp to a roped-off area where there was a circular parquet dance floor at the center of which, in the resounding echo that came down from the vaulted ceiling, you could almost hear the throaty voices of Carmen Mirandas who must have stood there. Across the lake was the Yacht Club, a vintage piece of modernism which, like the Guggenheim Museum, was no longer scandalous, but had even acquired with time a staid elegance and was vibrant with Oscar's playfulness and his strong sculptural sense. "Plastic form, in architecture," he wrote, "evolved as new techniques and new materials gave it different, innovative aspects. At first were the robust forms that construction in stone and brick required; then the arches, domes, and ogives, the broad spans, the free and unexpected forms that concrete permitted and modern themes solicited, sprang up." A few bends further along the lake was the glass chapel with the mural by Cândido Portinari whose earthy subject, a dog, had outraged the Church. But nowhere in Pampulha could I find even a hint of Oscar's militant socialism.

Somehow, contrary to his intentions, his utopia had ended up as a compound for the rich. The houses there were all mansions. One of his friends explained that he was only a "Platonic communist," while a critic dismissed him as "one rich Marxist," adding, "when did he ever design a poor man's house?"

In Brasília, Oscar's hopes for a fair society were reawakened. Here was a tabula rasa, a chance to break out of invidious molds and to create (to use Lewis Mumford's distinction) a "utopia of reconstruction" as opposed to one of escape. And in the beginning, during the building phase, it seemed as if it might work. "There were no barriers, just a mass of people— engineers, administrators, laborers alike—united in the same cause. At night we would all go to the same place, a shack called Olga's Bar, and dance in our muddy boots while someone flailed a guitar and others slapped tambourines and tapped their glasses and bottles. I would fall asleep in my hammock, dreaming of a better world. My deception came when Brasília was inaugurated. We had all worked together, but then the walls went up between the rich and the poor, and we stopped going to the same places. When I designed the apartments they told me that all people, rich and poor, would be able to live in them. But now only the rich can live in them. The poor cannot afford them. Twenty miles from Brasília the people have nothing. They see the beauty of Brasília through binoculars. It had seemed during the initial solidarity that the children of Brasília would grow without complexes, but instead it has become the most discriminatory city in Brazil. I see now that a social architecture without a socialist base leads to nothing, that you can't create a class-free oasis in a capitalist society, and that to try ends up being, as Engels said, a paternalistic pose that pretends to be revolutionary."

If Brasília failed to make a social revolution, it did nonetheless create an esthetic one. "You will not say that you have seen similar things anywhere else," Oscar said confidently. "For some it is function that is important in architecture. For me, it is beauty, fantasy, surprise." He spoke of a revelation he had while gazing at a blank wall, supported by two tiers of columns with elaborately scrolled capitals in the Doges' Palace in Venice. "The columns could have been simpler and more functional, but without those curves, they wouldn't have established such a splendid contrast with the vast, plain wall they were holding up. At that moment I realized that any form which creates beauty has a function.

"Of course if I had it to do again, I'd do a few things differently. I'd have more gardens, and a center where cars couldn't go. There is no real center in Brasília, as there is in Rio, where people can gather. And perhaps, too, I'd have given the buildings a few more stories, so there would be fewer roads. But these are minor points. The plan was good. Brasília is disciplined, and it has transcended the chaos and anarchy of other cities." I asked if he got up there much anymore. "Hardly ever," he said. "I am in friction with the military regime. In the last decade I've spent ten months of the year abroad. Most of my work has been in Italy, France, and Algeria." (Because of his communism his application to work in the United States had repeatedly been denied.) "A year ago I came back to do the Music Center. Now I'm president of an organization that is involved in the struggle for human rights. I say what I think because the government doesn't have the courage to shut me up." I asked about the long-barreled revolver beside his chair. He seemed embarrassed that I had noticed it. "Oh, it's nothing," he said with a nervous laugh.

In Brasília I didn't get the feeling the present government was any more of a fan of Oscar than he was of them. Shown into the office of Colonel Rubem Ludwig, President Geisel's press secretary, in Oscar's Planalto Palace, I made the mistake of saying, as an opener, "Well, it really makes sense, what Oscar was trying to do."

"Really," the colonel answered drily. "Tell me. I've never been able to figure it out."

———————————

Although Juscelino had wanted him to do the whole city, Oscar decided to concentrate on designing the public buildings, giving other architects the chance to develop the city plan. A competition was announced. Contestants for the Pilot Plan of Brasília should submit their entries within one hundred and twenty days. They would be judged by a panel that included Niemeyer, the president of NOVACAP, and a number of other Brazilian and European architects and city planners, the most famous of whom was Sir William Holford, head urbanist for the British government and planner of the capital of Rhodesia. The first price was a million cruzeiros. Twenty-six plans were entered, of which sixteen were quickly eliminated. Among the final ten was an elaborate presentation by Construtec, a firm in São Paulo that had involved its whole staff for several frantic months and spent four hundred thousand cruzeiros on colored graphics and a minutely detailed model of the proposed city made out of aluminum tubing. But the winner was Lúcio Costa, who spent just sixty-four hours and about twenty-five cruzeiros for pencils, paper, and an eraser.

Six years Oscar's senior, Costa lives on Leblon, a beach west of Copacabana. The mutual respect between the two men was deep; Oscar had described Lúcio as "a man of pure sensibility," and had insisted, as a prerequisite of our interview, that I speak with him first. It was no trouble setting up a meeting; there were no overprotective apprentices or overfull schedules to deal with, as had been the case with Oscar. It was simply a matter of finding his name in the phone book and giving him a call. "Just come," said the kind, patient voice at the other end. "Today, tomorrow, right now, if it's convenient." The man who opened the door had a pince-nez and a big, affable mustache like Albert Schweitzer's, and he was dressed in an old dark suit and tie. His apartment, with undifferentiated heaps of books and papers, fruit pits and paint cans in every corner, had surpassed conventional disorder; it was the quarters of a *distraído,* or distracted, Rio intellectual who had little concern for appearance. He settled into the threadbare sofa that seemed his thinking place. His eyes were shining tenderly and there was a profound simplicity about him. Soon a woman appeared with two demitasses of sweet black coffee.

"Brasília was really Kubitschek's creation," he began. "To modernize the country he launched a series of measures; he opened new iron mines, built up the Navy, attracted foreign industry, especially automotive. He constructed an arch of which Brasília was the keystone, keeping all the others in place. There were people who said it would never happen, but after twenty years the city has taken. It has streets, it has life, the daily *convivencia* of domestic and administrative life in a somewhat abstract world of forms. I think all of us involved in it had the sensation that a page of history was being turned. The last hundred years had been America's; now the world's century was beginning.

"But my part was hardly important. I didn't even see the site till it was laid out, and have only been there a few times since. It was Oscar who felt it was a thing of such importance that he gave up his friends and everything to live in the desert. When the competition was announced, each contestant received a copy of the Belcher Report. (I got the topographical information by reading it.) Of the five sites Brown was the poorest and least pleasant from the scenic point of view, but with the headwaters of three great rivers nearby, good for a lake. Sir William Holford, coordinator of the project, told me afterward that the first time he studied my text he couldn't make it out, because it was in Portuguese. 'The second time I understood, and the third time I was delighted,' he said. "My idea was the simplest, frankest, and clearest; and the result was *bonito,* too."

On the table before us was a postcard of an Amazonian Indian about to shoot an arrow into a river. "That's exactly it, the shape of my plan," he said, pointing to the X which the drawn bow formed with its projectile. "Basically," his presentation explained, "the plan arose from the primary gesture of one who marks or takes possession of a place: two axes crossing at right angles; the sign of the cross itself." The shape of Brasília is also frequently compared to an airplane, whose wings are folded slightly backward and slightly curved. The fuselage is bureaucratic, with the federal government at the nose and the district government at the tail. The wings, which are in fact called North Wing and South Wing, are residential. Along each wing sixty *superquadras,* or "superblocks," are laid out in a grid fifteen long by four deep. Each *superquadra,* fed by a winding cul-de-sac, is a mini-community of its own, with eighteen or so *blocos,* or apartment buildings, each six stories high, set on pilings, and separated by green spaces. "The ground will be carpeted with grass," the plan decreed, "and shrubs and foliage will screen the internal groupings of the *superquadra* from the spectator . . . and at the same time . . . will provide the inhabitants with shady avenues down which to stroll at leisure." To instill "pride of place" and a sense of identity Costa suggested that each *superquadra* be planted with a different species of tree. For every four *superquadras* there would be a primary school, a church, and an *interquadra,* a little shopping section with a grocery store, a hardware store, bakery, a supermarket, boutiques, and the like. With its parklike feeling and its self-sufficiency, the *superquadra* was patterned after the medieval town. It looked back to a time when communities were smaller and the quality of life supposedly better. Le Corbusier

39

had already tried to re-create the medieval environment in the town of Stevenage, England, in the 1920s, and the extreme rationality of Costa's plan, the orderly grid of even-storied buildings, was also indebted to the Frenchman. Having also worked on the Ministry of Education in 1936, Costa was an even more orthodox disciple of his than Niemeyer; the most prominently featured object in his apartment was a signed and dedicated Le Corbusier etching in the living room. When I asked if I could take his picture, Costa chose to pose before it. He would only allow me one snap. "Don't waste your film," he said, uncomfortably.

The homogeneity of the residential section would not only impart harmony and unity to the plan, but would, "while favoring the coexistence of social groups, avoid any undue and undesirable stratification of society." Apartments facing outward would naturally be more valuable than those looking into the *superquadra;* so would ones with frontage on a radial artery. These differences would allow a certain amount of classification "according to economic conditions in force at the time," but not so much as to deprive anyone of "that degree of comfort to which all members of society are entitled." Further differences would spring from variables in the density of residents per *bloco,* in the living space allotted each individual and each family, in the quality of building materials used, and the degree to which the structures were finished off. "The Development Company should, within the scope of the proposed outline plan, make provision for decent and economical accommodation for the entire population. The growth of slums, whether on the city outskirts or in the surrounding countryside, should at all costs be prevented." To make sure that everyone got to live in a *superquadra,* Costa urged that a governmental agency control the pricing and distribution of the apartments. He knew that if they were put on an open real estate market, speculation would begin, and the poor would be priced out of his city. After 1960, this is precisely what happened.

"You don't solve the social problems of a country by simply moving its capital," Costa explained. "And in Brazil the main problem is the huge base of poor in the population, of people who are not happy in their own land. Brasília was built by these people. They flocked to it because there was work and hope for a better life. But after the construction died down the population was a little disoccupied. Fifteen days after the workers came the grandmother, the mother, the whole family. But the original plan was for an administrative city of five hundred thousand, and there just wasn't room in it for all these people, most of whom had no experience with apartment-dwelling anyway. So the administration was faced with the problem of what to do with them. There were three possibilities. After the work was done, one third could be sent home. Since most of them were rural people another third could be put on outlying farms and grow food for the city. And the rest could be absorbed in the activities of the city. But this didn't work because when the work was over they didn't want to go back. As bad as they had it in Brasília, it was worse at home. And the model farms where the food was supposed to be grown became dachas for important figures in the government; you know how this sort of thing happens in Brazil. So the only solution was to create new nuclei, but well beyond the city limits, to avoid slums. These in time grew into satellite cities of their own."

East of the Pilot Plan, as if the plane were parting a cloud, would be a great V-shaped lake. Costa was adamant about what was to be done along its margins: "No housing will be permitted by the lake: the area must be kept unspoiled. The lakeshore will be treated as woodland and parkland, and green spaces over which the citizens may walk and enjoy other countryside amenities. Only sports clubs, restaurants, playing fields, swimming enclosures, and fishing clubs may operate around the lake." There were two reasons for this: Costa was aware how quickly lakes with houses around them become polluted, and he felt that the shoreline should be public domain, to be enjoyed by all. But human nature wants a house on the water, if it can afford one, and so this eminently sensible injunction would be ignored. Today the southern rim of Lake Paranoá is the splended Mansion Sector, the Scarsdale of Brasília. Niemeyer was incensed that the lake had been "usurped by the bourgeoisie."

At the heart of the city, where the wings joined the fuselage, Costa planned a Sector of Diversion to rival Piccadilly Circus, Times Square, and the Champs-Elysées. Here, too, fed by three levels of roads, would be the bus station. Perhaps the most innovative aspect of his plan was how he had applied the principles of highway engineering to ensure the unimpeded circulation of the city's traffic. Thanks to an elaborate network of ramps and cloverleafs there would be no intersections or streetcorners in Brasília and no stoplights except on the service roads. It would be a "speedway city." The pedestrians were diverted from the rushing cars by under- and overpasses. But "the separation of Man and Motor should not be taken to unnatural extremes," he was quick to add, "since it must not be forgotten that the car, today, is no longer man's deadly enemy; it has been domesticated and is almost a member of the family. It only becomes 'dehumanized' and resumes its hostile, threatening attitude, when it is reintegrated into the anonymous body of traffic." Perhaps he gave special thought to the transit system because, a few years earlier, his own wife had been killed in a car that he was driving.

Costa's Pilot Plan won over not only Niemeyer, Holford, and the other judges, but Juscelino. It had both the grandeur and the novelty—the sense of being a groundbreaking human experiment—which Juscelino felt were essential for the capital, yet it remained congenial. "While monumental," Costa explained, "the city is also comfortable, efficient, welcoming, and homey. It is at the same time spacious and neat, rustic and urban, imaginative and functional. It is not just an *urbs,* but a *civitas.*" I asked if he had ever thought of living there. "Me?" he answered. "Never. I'm a true son of Rio, though born in Toulon. I'm too *comodista,* addicted to the comforts here, to think of leaving." His building was the last on the beach, before the twin granite spires of a mountain called Two Brothers, whose basal slopes were velvet in the sunlight, rose out of the sea. At the foot of the building dark bodies were sprawled out on the sand, or were engaged in the delicate ballet of soccer and a variant of volleyball in which only the head and feet were allowed to touch the ball, or were bobbing and tumbling in the waves. You could tell it was a Catholic country, because many of the bathers would cross themselves before entrusting themselves to the surf. "Here a miracle is a miracle," Costa sighed. "That indolence . . . the beach at your door . . . no, I could never give it up."

Sifting through a stack of debris, he extracted a black-and-white photograph that showed two roads crossing on a barren prairie in the middle of nowhere. This was how Brown had looked late in 1956, when Costa first saw it. "I found the Planalto, that horizon without limit, excessively vast. It was out of scale, like an ocean, with immense clouds moving over it. By putting a city in the middle of it, we would be creating a landscape. In Brazil what makes a landscape are the architectonic masses, because most of it is desert." By then the first trip with material, including a gas generator and a radio telephone, had already been made. It took four days for the procession of jeeps and caterpillars to lumber there from Belo Horizonte. Oscar remembers how nice it was to wash the dust off his body in the rivers as the equipment was ferried across on rafts. About five miles from the city-to-be, on the edge of the largest patch of upland forest in the area, they threw up a little barracks for Juscelino and called it Catetinho, because it was a replica of the Catete, the presidential palace in Rio. After ten days of feverish work, on October 31, 1956, they cracked open a bottle of rum to celebrate its completion. But there was no ice, and the modern-day *bandeirantes* wondered how they were going to cool their drinks. Then, suddenly, the sky grew dark and they were pelted with hailstones the size of marbles. "Miracle! Miracle!" everyone shouted.

Oscar started roughing out the bureaucratic axis. Running downhill, it culminated in a natural bowl, and there he envisaged great slabs of glass rising up to the sky like the Pyramids, Stonehenge, or, more exactly, the United Nations Building, for which he had been a consultant a few years before. The sixteen ministries would be straight Le Corbusier, simple rectangular boxes marching two by two to the vanishing point. Behind them would be the Plaza of the Three Powers, where he would give tangible form to the triple nature of the government, with Executive, Legislative, and Judicial branches just like our own. Exactly how, he wasn't sure yet, but he knew it would express all that he felt about beauty, nobility, and inventiveness, and possibilities were already flooding his mind. He would be busy delivering the Monumental Sector, like a woman in the heat of labor, for the rest of the decade.

By early 1957 the desert of the Planalto Central had been converted to an immense, teeming construction site. Word of what was being done there had already spread, and workers from every part of Brazil were streaming in. By February somewhere in the region of three thousand workers were on the site. About two-thirds of the men who came at the beginning were young *nordestinos,* or northeasterners, with some experience in construction. Among them was Waldemar, the third child of José Leonias. He'd been the supply clerk at a construction yard in Floriano, verifying cargo manifests as trucks were unloaded and loaded. But he was twenty-two and raring to go, and hearing that there was good money to be made in Brasília, he threw a few clothes into a small leather suitcase with a wooden handle, and after reassuring his weeping mother that everything

44

would be all right, he took the ferry across the Parnaíba to the state of Maranhão, then a bus for two days to Imperatriz, where he boarded a small two-propeller plane that was going to Brasília. By the time he got there he had spent almost everything he had on the road, and was "almost at zero." He knew nobody, but then most of the other passengers on the plane were in the same situation. They all piled into jeeps and were taken to Cidade Livre, the frontier town that had sprouted spontaneously at the confluence of the two creeks a few miles from where Costa's Pilot Plan was already taking recognizable shape. Free City was as wild and lawless as Dodge City or any of the early settlements in the American West. When a particularly large brawl erupted in the red-light district, the cavalry was called out. Dismounting, they would march in a straight line up the central avenue, leading their horses behind them, and order would temporarily be restored. Cidade Livre consisted of three parallel avenues lined with ramshackle wooden structures of one or two stories. The latter, called *sobrados*, were derived from the shanty that evolved on the hillsides of Rio. The second story had more floor space and overlapped the first, so that its builder could make the most of his steep, limited terrain. The *sobrados* of Cidade Livre were built to be residences, but more often they were stores, with the merchandise on the ground floor and the owner living above, where he could keep an eye on it. When other satellite cities came to be built, other styles of *casa popular* were adopted. In the Federal District only Cidade Livre has samples of the colorful subrado architecture in quantity, rendered even more colorful with bright coats of blue, red, yellow, or green paint.

By 1958 the city boasted two thousand, six hundred commercial establishments, including a couple of dozen flophouses, one of which Waldemar checked into that night. There, to his amazement, he ran into a man he'd known in Floriano. "You won't believe it," the man said as they were lying in their bunks,

45

"but I've been making as much money here in a week as it took me two months to make back home." He was a brick mason. "They pay me by the wall. 'How long will this wall take you?' the boss asks. 'A day, a day and a half,' I tell him. 'So I'll pay you *two hundred cruzeiros,*'" the friend reported ecstatically.

The following morning both went to an office where work assignments were being handed out, and they were sent immediately to the dam. Sixteen square miles of river valley at the foot of the dome on which the Pilot Plan was rising were to be flooded, creating Lake Paranoá. The water level would be raised as high as twelve feet. The tranquil expanse of open water, with over seventy miles of shoreline, would provide a welcome break in the hot, itchy scrub. A small turbine at the dam would generate twenty-five thousand kilowatts of electricity, though most of the energy for the city, as well as the water, would be furnished by other dams north and upstream from the city. Numerous recreational possibilities would also be created. Another possible effect of the lake, that surface evaporation would ameliorate the local microclimate, has never been proven to everyone's satisfaction, because it flooded out the richest and most extensive forest on the Central Plateau, whose trees already provided, in the opinion of scientists who were critical of the project, as much moisture through transpiration as the lake would. So impressed with "this admirable mantle of forest" was the botanist on the Cruls Commission that he urged it "never be smitten by the ax of man."

An American firm, the Raymond Concrete Pile Company, had been hired to erect the steel frames of both the glass ministries and the dam. The awarding of this lucrative contract to foreigners, just as Brazil was struggling to realize its own steel-producing potential, was bitterly criticized in the Congress. Only the personal appearance of Niemeyer, who explained that the Americans had been hired for reasons of time and economy, placated the critics. Once installed, the gringos

were a further source of exasperation for Juscelino. They seemed
more concerned with their personal comfort, and to that end
spent several months putting up luxurious living quarters, than
with getting the job done in the record time they had promised.
If a piece of machinery broke down they were happy to have it
sent back to the United States for repair, which took three
months. They didn't understand the improvisational frontier
spirit of Brasília; they never got into its rhythm. Six months
before the inauguration Juscelino realized that the dam
wouldn't be ready in time, and called a hasty meeting of the
engineers. "How are we going to open the capital without its
lake?" he asked frantically. The prudent thing, he was told,
would be to wait till the dam was finished before bringing up the
water. You could bring up the water prematurely as high as the
dam had been completed, but you ran the risk of a sudden
rainstorm raising the water level and rupturing the whole
structure. With characteristic optimism, Juscelino went for the
second option. Waldemar was at the dam when he descended in
a helicopter that December. "How's it going?" Juscelino asked,
taking his hand. "He was very human," Waldemar remembers,
"but he was also in a hurry. The man wanted it ready." At
lunchtime he sat and ate with the workers. There was no
security. "He was a truly democratic person," a close friend of
Juscelino's recalled. "He could speak to anybody. The people
loved him because he embodied what they wanted the country
to be. He brought the country up, and the people rose, too."
Juscelino's frequent visits to the construction sites and his
personal appeals to the workers had a tremendous effect. Each
project had a sign in front of it with the date it had been started
and its deadline. Juscelino would come up to one of the men and
clap him on the shoulder. "What do you say, are you going to
give me this building by the deadline?" The man would usually
smile broadly and answer, "Why do you think I'm working so
hard?" And Juscelino would promise that if the man did the job

on time he would come back and give him a big hug. In his beguiling straightforwardness and his magnetism he resembled another indefatigable city-builder, Peter the Great. "He was interested in getting things done," Nigel Gosling wrote in a book called *Leningrad,* "and he mixed naturally with the people who did them."

Waldemar worked at the dam for two months as an *apontador,* assigning men to operate the machines. Soon after he had started, the summer rains began, and there were many days when it was impossible to work. The temperature in Brasília, at the low part of a meteorological cycle, in the late fifties was significantly lower than it is today, and some days it would go down to forty degrees. He had never felt such a *frio danado,* such a raw coldness, in Piauí. Other days, to keep on schedule, he worked a double shift, for twenty-four hours straight. Though many of the men who built Brasília worked night and day to make as much money as they could, there was only one serious accident at the dam. A black crane operator named Mosquito had lifted a huge block of concrete and was lowering it to the dam when the machine overturned with its weight and fell crashing into the gorge. Mosquito broke his back, shoulder and ribs, but miraculously lived. On Saturday night Waldemar and his friends would sometimes catch a ride to Cidade Livre, where they danced in bars to samba records spinning on generator-powered Victrolas. Fistfights were frequent, gunfights occasional, and almost always they were over a woman. Poverty was unknown. Everybody had money, and women to spend it on. On the rare Sundays he had off he would help friends put up their board-and-batten *barracas,* shacks on the edge of town, which they hoped by squatter's rights would entitle them to the land. Twice a month two trucks loaded with women, thoughtfully provided by NOVACAP, would call at the dam. The men would line up, and were given twenty minutes apiece.

A sense of mission began to swell in the breasts of the pioneers who were bringing Brasília to life, and somewhere in one of Cidade Livre's many bars an unknown philosopher began to describe himself and his fellows as a *candango*. The word was already in use, but the application was new. It seems to be derived, like many words in Brazilian Portuguese, from *bundo*, a collective term for the various dialects which the slaves brought over from Africa. In Angola, where many Bantus were abducted, *ca* meant little, and *ndong* darling, but *ndongo* also meant a large canoe. The word first appears in Brazil as a derogatory term used by the slaves for their Lusitanian captors. Then it became a subcategory of the racial epithet, *cafuzo*. Most of the rural population was pure black, mulatto (a mixture of white and black), *cafuzo* (black and Indian), or *mameluco* (white and Indian). A *candango* was a cross between a *mameluco* and a black; in other words, he was two parts African, one part Indian, and one Portuguese. Since the appearance of many, if not their actual blood mixture, seemed to be *candango*, it gradually came to describe the participants in the periodic rural exoduses that took place in Brazilian history. It meant a down-and-out drifter, comparable to the North American "Okie" or "fruit tramp," as the migrant laborer is known in central Florida. But now, instead of it being a term of disparagement, instead of being ashamed to be *candangos*, the builders of Brasília suddenly became proud of their humble background and their heroic role in this great event. Today the meaning of *candango* is in the process of shifting from the pioneer who built the city, to someone born there, who is also called a *Brasiliense*. A *candango* is to Brasília as a *carioca* is to Rio. In the Leonias family Waldemar is a bonafide *candango*, because he came to Brasília before the inauguration; so are fourteen of Dona Joana's grandchildren, so far, who are Brasília-born. A kindergarten in one of the *superquadras* of the South Wing is called the *Candanginho*, and two bronze *Candangos* sculpted by Bruno Giorgi stand in the Plaza of the Three Powers. They are about thirty feet tall and very futuristic, like the humanoids who descend from the spaceship in the movie *Close Encounters of the Third Kind.*

The phase between 1957 and 1960 is usually labeled "the battle of construction" in the various booklets one picks up on newsstands in Brasília or at the Department of Tourism. The sound of gears grinding and hammers pounding, of draglines and graders, bulldozers and sheepsfoot rollers, was continuous. When the sun went down, light generators went on, and when it returned, the generators went off; but the activity never ceased. To American journalist Emily Hahn, Brasília, which she visited late in 1959, a few months before its inauguration, seemed "like a colony of coral that is breaking through the surface as an atoll." Some of the buildings went up in fifteen days, Oscar told me. Because of the time factor eleven identical glass boxes, ten stories high and wider than they were tall, were built for the ministries. The only internal fixtures were the sanitary facilities at either end and an elevator shaft at the center. Each ministry partitioned its building according to its needs. Amazingly, in spite of the haste, it all held together. There was nothing as embarrassing as the cracks that appeared in the Lyndon Baines Johnson Library soon after its construction. The first primary school, a Niemeyer project, was opened on October 18, 1957, its construction having begun twenty days earlier, and received an immediate enrollment of three hundred children of engineers and NOVACAP functionaries. The first secondary school, which now has eight thousand students, was built in sixty-six days. Juscelino thanked the architect, Zerbi Lins, personally. Lins lives now in a comfortable apartment in Bloco E, Superquadra 112 South. "I love Brasília because I saw it grow," the remarkably fit and youthful fifty-seven-year-old Lins said. He knew Oscar slightly, but because they were both working fourteen hours a day they didn't have time to socialize.

For the less important structures Oscar would often give a verbal description of their esthetic ideal, make a few rough sketches, and leave the details to people like Lins. Lins personally supervised the construction of fifteen voltage-reduction substations, eleven stores in the Southern Commercial Sector, five hundred houses for the engineers along W-3, the main service road; the waterlines for Sobradinho, one of the satellite cities; and participated in the erection of several ministries and *blocos*. On the job by seven, he worked twelve hours straight, pausing only for a quick snack of biscuits, milk, and two eggs; at seven a jeep would take him home for dinner, after which he would return to work and remain there till midnight, though on a few occasions he worked straight through the night. Like Waldemar he spoke highly of the solidarity among the *candangos,* and described Juscelino as "a fabulous man of vision. Once I walked into a big crowd. I thought it was a fight, but it was Juscelino being embraced by dust-covered workers."

I picked up a shot of Juscelino snapped to attention with a small, dark, bearded and bemedaled man whom I recognized as Emperor Haile Selassie of Ethiopia. The visit of the illustrious Lion of Judah, in December 1960, after the inauguration, ended up a comedy of errors. The multititled autocrat was the first reigning sovereign to come to Brazil since King Albert of Belgium in 1922, and Juscelino had prepared an elaborate reception for him. But at the airport there was an embarrassing scuffle between an Air Force officer and a cinematographer in plain view of the King of Kings. They were standing at attention, Juscelino and the Negus, as the national anthem was being played; it was at this moment that Lins took their picture, and Lins claims that as he was lowering his camera, the president winked at him. Then the two heads of state got into a limousine in which, as Juscelino would report years later, the Negus, speaking in French, revealed that he was about to convert his country from an absolute to a constitutional monarchy, with a parliament, and that his chief priority was to educate his people. The limousine pulled up in front of the Planalto Palace, the office of the chief executive in the Plaza of the Three Powers. Juscelino was especially proud of its architecture and that of the Dawn Palace, the presidential residence, from which it was derived. When Oscar had brought him his first design for the Dawn Palace, Juscelino felt it lacked the requisite monumentality; he sent him back to the drawing board with some misgiving, because he had never rejected an idea of Oscar's before. "I want something that will still be admired a hundred years from now," he told him. The second design was grand and lyrical, capricious and imposing. Oscar had achieved an appearance of weightlessness by enclosing the glass structure with delicate columns of white marble that flared out dramatically at their base, so that the building seemed to be born aloft on sails. A ceremonial ramp led to the second floor of the Planalto Palace and up it Juscelino and the Prince of Princes, with a lion skin thrown over one shoulder, now proceeded. One of the Ethiopian entourage, replete with decorations, walked into a barely visible glass wall and crumpled to the floor. Once everyone was safely inside the palace, the emperor attempted to fasten the Necklace of Queen Saba, the highest order of his land, about Juscelino's neck, but it suddenly broke and fell to the floor. Both statesmen stooped to pick it up, and according to Lins, who was standing in the balcony, knocked heads. The ceremony was suspended while the decoration was taken out for repair, and during the lull an aide approached the king and whispered something in his ear that upset him visibly. After the ceremony was over he drew Juscelino aside and said, "A bulletin has just come from Addis Ababa informing me that

52

there has been a military coup in the capital, and that I am no longer the king of Ethiopia." Juscelino gasped, and Selassie went on with admirable control, "I am waiting for confirmation of the bulletin, and as soon as I receive it, I will let your excellency know." A few hours later he notified Juscelino that his son, Prince Asfa Wassen, had apparently made a speech urging the people to recognize the coup. "I know my son," Selassie said, "and I don't believe he would ever be capable of such treason." Juscelino asked if he would rather the gala state banquet which had been readied for that evening were canceled, and Selassie said, "Absolutely not! I wouldn't think of it, after all the trouble you've gone to. But there is a favor you could do for me." Whereupon he produced a check for sixty thousand dollars that he had just made out, signing himself as the emperor of Ethiopia. Juscelino was in a bind. He hadn't the funds to cash the check personally, and how could he authorize the State Department to endorse it if the emperor had really been deposed? With the greatest reluctance, State finally endorsed the check. A few days later Selassie marched triumphantly into Addis Ababa, freed his son, who had made the speech under duress, and had the leaders of the rebellion, Generals Dibon and Wendafrash, publicly executed. Then he cabled Juscelino with the news, that he could rest easy, because the check was covered.

Brasília received many other notable visitors around its time of completion. Yuri Gagarin, who had recently returned from outer space, said, "I feel as if I have just disembarked on another planet, not earth." Aldous Huxley, with his concern for what the world was coming to and his deep sympathy with Latin America, had to see it. He wrote in August 1958, "I came directly from Ouro Prêto to Brasília. What a dramatic journey across time and history. A journey from Yesterday to Tomorrow, from what has ended to what will begin, from old realizations to new promises." Frank Capra, the filmmaker, hailed it as the eighth wonder of the world. Queen Elizabeth asked why the presidential residence was called the Palace of Dawn, to which Juscelino replied, "I chose the name myself. What else will Brasília be, your majesty, if not the dawn of a new day for Brazil?" The ubiquitous Nelson Rockefeller was also there. So were Prince Mikasa; Cardinal Montini, the future Pope Paul VI, Presidents Gronchi, Salazar, López Mateos, and Stroessner, of Italy, Portugal, Mexico, and Paraguay, respectively; the Duchess of Kent; and Fidel Castro. The visit of President Eisenhower, a month before the inauguration, came at a time when Panamerican relations were at an all-time low ebb. Two years earlier Vice-President Nixon had been hissed in Lima and stoned in Caracas. The red carpet rolled out to Eisenhower's plane proved too long. There was a delay during which someone suggested that the pilot be asked to withdraw the plane and make a new approach, whereupon a nearby *candango* produced a knife and hacked off the excess carpet. The president stepped out, but because his plane had arrived a half hour early on a tailwind, Juscelino was not yet there to meet him. Fortunately neither president was one to stand on ceremony.

For Oscar, the critical visitor was Le Corbusier, in whose honor a grove of buriti palms was planted. He praised his disciple for the city's inventiveness. "I think often of you and your magnificent work," he wrote later. "Bravo!" But it was another Frenchman, André Malraux, de Gaulle's minister of culture, whose visit had the greatest impact on the capital itself. He came on August 29, 1959, and his speech was not only a distinguished piece of Gallic oratory but a lucid analysis of Brasília's significance as the element that would unify the country and usher in a new era of Brazilian history. Some of his words seemed to echo the Belcher Report: "Almost all the great cities have arisen spontaneously, around a privileged place. What History contemplates with us today is the emergence of the first edifices of a city created by the will of one man and the hope of a nation. If the old passion for inscribing monuments should ever be reborn, the following words should be engraved: Audacity, Energy, and Faith." By the final sentence hardly a person in the audience was not moved. "And in your great funereal night a murmur of glory accompanies the pounding of the anvils that salute your audacity, your faith, and the destiny of Brazil, as the Capital of Hope surges on!" This inspiring term, the Capital of Hope, became Brasília's official sobriquet, while the bold columns of the Palace of Dawn became the city's logo and, later, the symbol of the new Brazil. Twenty years afterward, Iraci Leonias' fourth-grade class in Sobradinho, with neat blue uniforms and hands folded across their desks, sang me the hymn of Brasília. It is called "The Capital of Hope," and their rendition of it was spirited:

> In the middle of an untamed virgin land,
> In the most splendorous of dawns,
> Happy as a child's smile,
> A dream transformed itself into reality,
> The most fantastic city came into being,
> Brasília, the Capital of Hope.

Later in his visit, when Juscelino and Malraux were alone, looking at the city from a balcony in the Planalto Palace, Malraux seized his arm and asked, "Tell me, how did you ever manage to do all this in a time of open democracy? I thought such things were possible only under a dictatorship."

On December 6, 1956, Juscelino inaugurated the airport, with a mile and a half of paved runway. Three months later the first mass was held at the highest point in the city, and a simple wooden cross erected on the spot. The cross is still there, and a nearby sector of *superquadras,* Cruzeiro, is named for it. The mass was attended by some fifteen thousand people, and conducted by the archbishop of São Paulo, Dom Carlos Carmelo de Vasconcelos Motta, who predicted that Brasília would be "the magic trampoline for the integration of Amazonia into the national life." The way to do this was to open the area up with roads. The road from Belo Horizonte to Brasília, with one hundred and fifty paved miles, had been open since January. Now Juscelino conceived an epic road-building project comparable to the construction of the Alcan Highway or the transcontinental railroad of the previous century: a highway a thousand miles long from Brasília to Belém, at the mouth of the Amazon. The Belém-Brasília was three years in the making. From the air it looked like a red thread running dead straight through the Green Hell of the rain forest. It was the backbone of Juscelino's highway system, from which lateral roads, notably the Transamazon, would shoot out and "recuperate areas asphyxiated by the want of paths of communication." Its builders had much to contend with: mosquito-born malaria, mud, torrential rain and torrential rivers, the deadly fer-de-lance, the unsuspected irregularity of the terrain under the trees, the rock-hardness of the immense trees themselves. Although the Indians never attacked, one sensed that they were always near at hand, watching. Provisions and equipment, even live cattle, were airlifted to the front line where feverish slashing extended the road about a half mile a day. The workers felt as if they were ravishing a sanctuary, and that sooner or later someone would have to pay for it. Only two weeks before the road was to be inaugurated, on January 15, 1959, a tree fell and crushed to death Bernard Sayão, the herculean man Juscelino had put in charge of the operation. The jungle had its revenge and in the process it gave Brasília a martyr. A year later Juscelino got the idea of having a "Caravan of National Integration" made up of Mercedes trucks, Ford and Volkswagen sedans, and Willys and Unimog jeeps, all manufactured in Brazil, run the entire length of the Belém-Brasília. This would demonstrate the strides that were being made on several fronts of national endeavor, both the road-building program and the Brazilian automobile industry, which Juscelino was working hard to develop. The caravan took a week to complete its mission. There were no serious mishaps, though some of the wider rivers were not yet bridged and the vehicles had to be floated across on oil-drum rafts. Today the edges of the highway are a burnt-out wasteland. All the forest in sight of the road has gone up in smoke and been converted to third-rate and short-lived cattle country, while the rest of Amazonia, for the most part, remains as unintegrated as ever.

By October 1958, a hundred and forty-three *blocos,* with a total of about six thousand apartments, with between nine hundred fifty and two thousand square feet of floor space and from two to four rooms apiece, were under construction. Five thousand three hundred and one civil servants, mostly in the employ of the military, the treasury, and the three branches of government, were already living and working in the new capital. The final structures of the Monumental Sector, which Oscar would number among his definitive works, had begun to take form: the stained-glass cathedral, a corolla with curved stems of poured concrete that represented the states of Brazil holding aloft the cross; the Palace of Congress, whose twin glass towers, twenty-eight stories each, housing the offices of senators and deputies, were the tallest buildings in Brasília and served as a proud reminder that the government was, above all, a constitutional democracy (an aspect of the city's architecture that hasn't been pointed out in the tourist booklets for the past decade and a half); and the Municipal Theater, a majestic, gradually tapering pyramid inspired by the Mayan temples. After a few months Waldemar, who had come at the tail end of the battle, was transferred from the dam to the bus station, where he was exposed to his first escalator. Then he worked on a cinema in the South Wing and in 1960, taking a short vacation from construction, he participated in a door-to-door census of the *barracas* that had sprouted by the hundreds in the precincts of the Pilot Plan. "Ninety percent were *nordestinos,*" he recalled, "the most ignorant element. The people had much anger, much agony."

Nineteen fifty-eight was a year of calamitous drought in the Northeast. These *secas,* or dry spells, are cyclical; every few decades comes a bad one. Rivers vanish, vegetation shrivels, cattle die en masse, and the whole Northeast becomes a furnace. In 1897 twenty thousand *flagelados,* or drought victims, starved at the gates of Fortaleza, the capital of Ceará, because there was no food for them. In March 1958, about ten thousand *flagelados* began to leave the Northeast in a great diaspora. About half of them, barefooted, emaciated, with only the rags on their backs and a few crusts of bread, descended on Cidade Livre and created Brasília's first *favela,* throwing up precarious *barracas* of old wood, flattened cans, cement sacks, and scrounged sheets of corrugated zinc. A *favela* is a haphazard urban slum without an infrastructure of water, sewage, or electric lines, and it was precisely what Costa had tried to exclude from the Federal District. "The city was idealized to perfection," a journalist in Brasília told me. "What is deforming it is population pressure, internal migration." Before long the *flagelados* were threatening to march en masse on the Pilot Plan with demands for work, food, housing, and health care, and NOVACAP realized that it had a problem. Only the speech of Ernesto Silva, president of NOVACAP, who got up on a kerosene can in front of the angry swarm, averted the confrontation. He said that a city with stores, schools, a hospital, and an industrial college, was being created for them. Lots had been measured off, to which NOVACAP would transport them free of charge and there help them put up provisional housing. Reluctantly the *flagelados* accepted the idea. The city was about ten miles from Brasília; NOVACAP wanted this distance so its effluent wouldn't drain into the Paranoá basin, already being polluted by Cidade Livre, and also to discourage future marches on the capital. And so the first of the Federal District's satellite cities came into being. It was called Taguatinga, after the creek that ran through it. Many places in Brazil are called Taguatinga, a Tupi-Guarani Indian word that means "white clay bank" and, by transference, "white village."

Waldemar saw many *favelas* speedily tacked into being and just as quickly taken down. One of the shantytowns, Vila Planalto, grew up five hundred yards from the Dawn Palace, around a group of well-constructed wooden houses for the engineers, and spread quickly into the valley that was to be flooded by Lake Paranoá. Waldemar was living there at the time, and he remembers that after the city was ready, Juscelino came and tried to persuade them to go home. "Everyone told him, 'I'm not going. I'm a *candango.*' Then Juscelino said, 'Okay, I won't bring in the police, but soon the dam will be closed and you will have to move.'" Many of the *barracas* were flooded and the rest torn down. But no one went home. They found a place to live in Taguatinga or one of the other satellite cities that was growing up. More than any other city in the country, Brasília has managed to keep on top of its *favela* problem by nipping it in the bud, though scattered hovels persist, some only a short walk from the Monumental Sector. By April 21, 1960, the city was ready. The principal roads were open, and three thousand, eight hundred apartments inhabited; the telephone system, built in a record time of ninety days, boasted five thousand lines, eight completely automated substations, plus twenty-three switchboards with four thousand, one hundred and twenty extensions in the main public buildings. The population was about a hundred thousand, a figure of which Juscelino could not help feeling proud when he compared it with the hundred and twenty-six civil servants who had reluctantly packed their bags and come down from Philadelphia to populate Washington in time for its inauguration. The two hundred thousand guests who poured into Brasília for its inauguration were a fair cross-section of the society, including socialites from Rio with the latest fashions from Paris and newly contacted Indians from Amazonia, fully regaled with body paint and ceremonial feathers. Among the guests was my neighbor in Westchester County, Mrs. Richard Momsen; her husband was the first American lawyer to be accredited in Brazil, and her son, co-author of the previously mentioned geography of Brazilian development. She remembers how the edges of her long dress were stained with red dust. Because there was no room in the Plano, as the Pilot Plan, or Brasília proper, was already being called, she had to stay in Cidade Livre. Personal friends of the Kubitschek family, numbering in the hundreds, were put up in the Palace of Dawn. At the inaugural ball in the Planalto Palace, before starting the first dance, Juscelino made a short speech: "Three years ago, on this very spot, a wolf crossed in front of my car. His eyes became phosphorescent in the headlights. Today, I receive three thousand guests in tails." Earlier in the day the first newspaper in the capital had come out with its maiden edition. It took the name *Correio Brasiliense* after the long-defunct paper whose owner had urged, in 1813, the interiorization of the capital. "We are no longer those crabs," the lead editorial proclaimed, "scratching the sands of the coastal beaches, of which the ancient chronicler spoke, but a people which has projected itself into the heart of the continent, which has taken its territory virilly in its hands and is preparing to be, in a short while, one of the four great nations of the universe." Waldemar participated in the parade of the *candangos,* who marched in loose but proud formation down the esplanade of the ministries. Up on the hill, where only a few months before he had lived in a tent until the bus station's viaduct was completed, he now saw huge, illuminated blow-ups of the "Three Musketeers," as they were called—Kubitschek, Niemeyer, and Costa—as well as of Ber-

nard Sayão, the martyr, and Israel Pinheiro, the president of
NOVACAP, leader of the army of *candangos,* and soon to be the
first governor of Brasília. There was a ceremony in which
Juscelino received the gold key to the city from Pinheiro,
thanked the *candangos,* and said he was proud to be one of them.
At 9:45, mass was celebrated in the cathedral of His Most
Reverend Eminence, Cardinal Dom Manuel Gonçalves Cere-
jeira, the papal legate. As he held the chalice up to the altar, the
band of the Corps of Naval Fusiliers broke out with the national
anthem, and at that moment it was noticed that Juscelino, in
the first pew, was covering his face with one hand and sobbing
uncontrollably. The battle was over. So, effectively, was
Juscelino's political career. He had another ten months in office;
after that, though no one knew it yet, and though he would
remain Brazil's most popular public figure, he would never
again play a central role in the national life of his country.
Juscelino's tears were contagious and soon everyone in the
cathedral was crying. Waldemar was milling in the throng
outside when suddenly dozens of spotlights were thrown on, and
Oscar and Lúcio's shimmering city, scarcely believable then
and still extremely modern today, was flooded with light. And
all night long there were fireworks. Waldemar says he had never
seen anything like it.

Part Two

Niemeyer and Costa had provided a dramatic setting, and drama was now to follow. On January 31, 1961, Juscelino passed the presidential sash to his successor, Jânio da Silva Quadros. A large, euphoric crowd saw the new chief of state, who had been elected by a landslide, installed in the new capital. Thin, mustachioed Quadros was a messianic character, intelligent but unstable. Having been the governor of São Paulo, where perhaps 70 percent of Juscelino's industrial boom had taken place, he got credit for his jurisdiction's sudden leap forward and was tremendously popular. But with Juscelino no longer at the helm, everything soon seemed to fall apart. The biggest problem was inflation. Brasília alone had already cost about five hundred million dollars by the inauguration and was ultimately expected to run about two billion, or higher than the country's entire annual budget. Its total cost has been the subject of at least one scholarly paper, but because private *empresários* took over much of the construction after 1960, the exact figure will probably never be known. "I seem to remember that a figure of forty billion cruzeiros was often mentioned in the early sixties," one of the most successful of the *empresários* told me. "But those were old cruzeiros, the equivalent of forty million today, multiplied by the 1500 percent inflation we've experienced since 1960." During Juscelino's administration the cruzeiro plunged from sixty-five to two hundred to the dollar, and by August, when Jânio Quadros renounced the presidency, it had dropped a hundred more. Quadros' official reason for resigning after only eight months in office was that "occult forces" had prevented him from governing the way he wanted to; but many people close to the political scene at that time believe that he wanted more power than a democracy would let him have, and that the renunciation was only a maneuver to provoke a political crisis which he was hoping would prompt the people to call him back and invest him with the authority of a dictator. "But the Brazilian people were smart enough to see through his bluff," a woman privy to Quadros' machinations told me, "and they didn't call him back. Had the economy been more stable, he could have been a big leader, for better or worse. He wanted to be a messiah." During the abortive regime of Jânio Quadros the construction of Brasília ground to a complete halt. Only one project, Niemeyer's dovecote in the Plaza of the Three Powers, got finished. But it is a splendid dovecote, like a sixty-foot-high concrete clothespin stood on end, and the pigeons seem to like it, for hundreds of them roost there.

The vice-president, João Goulart, was touring China when news of Quadros' abdication reached him, and he hurried back to Brazil in time to be sworn in on September 7. As the head of the Labor Party who had amassed a sizable fortune cattle-ranching in the South, Goulart had been a well-known political leader during the time of Kubitschek. Many felt that he would have been quite happy to remain vice-president and that he considered it more important to retain the leadership of his party than to be president. His showing, at any rate, was no more competent than that of his predecessor. Inflation continued to rise stupendously and was aggravated by strikes and riots which, since they were organized by activists in his own party, Goulart was powerless to stop. Goulart himself spent

most of his time in Rio waging an internecine battle for control
of the Labor Party with his brother-in-law, Leonel Brizola. The
consolidation of Brasília was one of the last things on his mind.
Construction there proceeded fitfully, paralyzed by shortages.
Three times the banks closed, and on one occasion, when they
didn't open for seventeen days, the *empresários* had to fly the
payroll in for their workers, who were threatening to riot.
Sometimes food ran out and people had to stand in line for
things like sugar. A columnist from the Trinidad *Sunday Guardian*
who visited the capital in 1962 described it as "a ghost town
populated by very reluctant ghosts." Through the 1960s the
general consensus among the government functionaries and
foreign diplomats stationed in Brasília was that the city would
not last more than twenty years, after which it would be
abandoned, like the deserted ceremonial cities of the Aztecs and
the Mayans, and there would only be ruins for their children to
see. Meanwhile the national crisis deepened. Many feared that
Goulart was leading the country toward communism; they were
frightened by the extremity of Brizola's agrarian reform bill,
which Goulart had accepted in order to keep the Labor
leadership. By early 1964 the situation in Brazil had become
nearly anarchic, and there are few, even the staunchest enemies
of the present regime, who will deny that something desperate
had to be done to return the country to order. Goulart's leftist
leanings had alarmed not only his countrymen, but the American ambassador to Brazil, Lincoln Gordon, who by 1963 had
become convinced that Goulart was planning to overthrow the
constitution and set up a proletarian dictatorship in the manner
of his mentors, Getúlio Vargas and Juan Perón. If this happened, Gordon warned, Brazil would certainly fall to communism. There was already plenty for a patriotic American
observer to be worried about, like Miguel Arraes, the governor
of Pernambuco and a strident communist, who had been calling
for the seizure of all American holdings in Brazil and the

expulsion of all "gringo imperialists" from the country. Whether Gordon and other members of the American Embassy had any direct connection with the military resistance movement that by late March 1964 was beginning to crystallize around General Humberto de Alencar Castelo Branco, is still debated. As regularly as the charge has been made since the coup, Gordon and the State Department have denied it. According to Gordon, "the movement was one hundred percent purely Brazilian," and while he has conceded that he believed Goulart to be "the greatest danger to his country's democracy," he emphasized that "there is a critical distinction between awareness and participation." But the evidence would seem to point to an involvement.

In 1978, Gordon had admitted that the CIA poured money into Brazilian political fronts to support candidates against the Labor Party in the 1962 elections, though he said he "would be amazed" if the amount was anything like the twenty million dollars mentioned by A. J. Languth in his book *Hidden Terrors*. Documents only declassified that year revealed that an American naval task force composed of an aircraft carrier, six destroyers, and four oil tankers was dispatched to Brazilian waters on March 31, 1964, and ordered to turn back on April 2, when the rapid success of the coup made its presence unnecessary. Confronted with these documents, Gordon explained that the task force "was intended to make possible a limited form of American action in a particular hypothetical contingency, a civil war with Brazil divided on geographic lines, the forces evenly matched, and with one side recognized by us. In that hypothesis, the task force would have had three purposes: (a) to provide logistical support, especially in petroleum products, to the side we believed to represent moderation and democracy; (b) to discourage the opposing side through the showing of the American flag on a powerful vessel; and (c) to assist if necessary in the evacuation of American citizens from regions involved in civil combat."

Whatever the American role, the coup took place, Goulart was packed off to exile in Uruguay, and few people in Washington regretted that he had been deposed. If there was a CIA involvement, the agency helped deal a blow to democracy from which Brazil has yet to recover, and America's subsequent stand on human rights there takes on an almost perverse dimension. Clandestine CIA activity is a favorite topic in the Brazilian press, and many Brazilians are convinced that the United States in April 1964 was planning an intervention on the scale of its invasion of the Dominican Republic the following year. "The trouble with U.S. policy toward Latin America," said a Brazilian who felt that Goulart was merely a victim of events beyond his control and had none of the totalitarian aspirations attributed to him by Gordon, "is that it is simplistic. They think that everybody south of the Rio Grande is the same. But we are not a radical people, and if we had been left to our own problems, we would have solved them. We would never go the way of Fidel."

The hearty congratulations that Gordon persuaded President Johnson to write to the Supreme Revolutionary Command, as the military leaders of the coup called themselves, were followed by expressions of "serious concern" several months later as it became clear that the generals had no intention of calling a national election in the visible future or of relinquishing their authority to civilian hands, as the Army had always done in the past whenever it had been necessary for it to step in and help a change of regime go smoothly. Traditionally, as Gilberto Freyre, one of the country's eminent historians, had explained in 1945, the Army was "the inheritor of the constitutional role that during long years the crown of the emperor had played in the Brazilian political system. . . . [It continues] to be ready to act in a suprapartisan way if such action is absolutely necessary to restore law and order." And indeed General Castelo Branco had promised to step in only for a short while, until order was restored and a new election could be called. But others in the

Army, whom Castelo Branco was unable to curb, had different intentions. "Democratic procedure went by the board last week," the *Newsweek* correspondent reported on April 20. The junta began by jailing five thousand "enemies of democracy" without right to a lawyer or to appeal in their own defense. Some were clearly communists, but some were clearly not. Thirty-nine deputies and one senator were expelled from the Congress, and fifty-eight notable figures in Brazilian public life, including ex-presidents Quadros and Goulart, were stripped of their political and civil rights. In June, Juscelino, still the most popular politician in Brazil, was also deprived of his rights, and he immediately flew to Spain for a three-month lecture tour from which he would not return for six years. The rest of that decade was an ugly time for Brazil. Artistic creativity and the freedom of self-expression were stifled by extensive censorship of all the media. The Policia Militar broke into homes and bars and tales of torture and beatings at police stations and in prisons were reported everywhere, but never to strangers, even to taxi drivers, for you never knew who was an undercover agent. Waldemar remembers that the police in Brasília at that time were constantly breaking up groups and telling everyone to move on, even though they had only been talking about private matters. One of his sister Marie José's students in Floriano, a handsome and intelligent young man named Audi, came down to Brasília in 1968 and there, at the newly opened university, got involved with a subversive crowd. The group was discovered to have an arsenal of stolen weapons, and Audi was sent to prison. A reporter interviewed him behind bars and asked why he had stolen the arms. "I didn't steal them," he said. "I disappropriated them from the bourgeoisie." Audi was released in 1971 and returned to Floriano to see his mother. After a day there he disappeared, and no one has heard from him since. Almost everyone knew someone who disappeared during the height of the purges, and one woman told me that in 1965 she even witnessed a summary execution. A young pupil at the fashionable American school in Rio, she happened to be at recess when an ambulance followed by a police van stopped at the crest of a nearby ridge. Two policemen got out of the van, opened the back, took out a blindfolded, handcuffed man, drew their revolvers, and shot him point-blank. Then white-uniformed attendants got out of the ambulance, placed him on a stretcher, and drove away.

General Castelo Branco's power ebbed steadily until he was only a puppet of the junta. Early in 1967 there was a revolution within the revolution and he was overthrown by General Artur de Costa e Silva. Under his direction governmental repression reached its peak; his cohorts in the Army, Air Force, and Marines were unwilling to relinquish any power to civilians, and for the last eleven months of his administration, until he died in office of a cerebral hemorrhage on October 30, 1969, there was no Congress, even though for five years the Congress had been like the Duma of Czar Nicholas II, a powerless advisory body which the head of state was free to dissolve whenever it irritated him. "With the advantage of hindsight," Lincoln Gordon would concede fourteen years after the initial coup, "I can justly be accused of naiveté in believing that constitutional democracy would be restored after a short period of emergency."

The closing of the Congress had a dire effect on the still struggling status of the new capital. Under Castelo Branco the rhythm of construction (after an initial hesitation about whether to adopt the city at all) had picked up for the first time since Juscelino. But under Costa e Silva the rhythm was lost again. There were nine stoppages due to political problems. Without a Congress investors there lost faith in the city. "The big lung of Brasília," an investor explained, "is the Congress. When representatives from all over the country are living and working here, you have faith in the city." With the accession of Emilio Garrastazú Médici to the presidency the situation in Brasília began to look up again. Brazil was getting back on its feet economically. Médici was more outgoing than his austere predecessor, and for the first time the city began to acquire the semblance of a social life. The new president gave much of his attention to making Brasília the true capital. He completed a railroad to São Paulo and its seaport, Santos; he built a huge indoor sports arena that bears his name, and other centers of leisure. He improved roads and transport to the satellite cities and added the Transamazon to the national highway-building agenda. He reopened the Congress, eased up on the censorship and repression a bit, and, most importantly, in 1973 he required the entire government and all the foreign embassies to be in Brasília. It was this last measure that finally consolidated the capital. In 1963 only sixty deputies were living in Brasília—the other four hundred-plus were still in Rio—and only a handful of foreign countries had outposts there. Until 1973 conversation at diplomatic dinners and bureaucratic cocktail parties in Brasília consisted mainly of the participants commiserating with each other over the misfortune of having to be there. Every weekend planes would fly the unfortunate senators, deputies, and diplomats home to Rio. But by 1974 a great change could be noted in the capital. Brasília had finally caught on. Investors began to believe in it again, and there was feverish speculation as the price of lots in the Mansion Sector rose overnight from forty thousand to 1.5 million cruzeiros. Only a short while before one could take the main arteries at ninety miles per hour and be confident of meeting no more than one car every twenty minutes. Now automobiles started to come in at the rate of a thousand a month, and by 1976 there were traffic jams four times a day in the Southern Commercial Sector, in the morning, evening, and twice at lunchtime. Médici's successor, Ernesto Geisel, brought many of his projects to conclusion and appointed as governor of the Federal District an engineer who could cope with the problems of the mushrooming city. He also put out the word to the Army and the police that the days of wanton brutality were over. By the time the Carter Administration made its plea for the upholding of human rights in Brazil, Geisel had already, at great political risk to himself, fired his own minister of war, a particularly brazen offender, and Brazilian-American relations, having fared well under Kissinger, were set back by the well-intentioned but belated gesture, which many Brazilians felt was a reversion to the old condescending paternalism. Under Geisel Brazil returned to stability for the first time in over a decade, and it was time to think of giving back to the people a voice in what was happening. Brazilians are an exceptionally passive, unpolitical, and light-hearted people, but even they were getting tired of the iron hand with which the junta had been ruling the country for fifteen years. In September 1978 Geisel repealed Institutional Act 5b, which had given the president extraordinary power, in 1964, to revoke the political rights of citizens, to dismiss congressmen and Supreme Court justices theretofore appointed for life, and to close the Congress by declaring a state of national emergency. In January 1979, when we arrived in Brasília on our last visit, Geisel had just liberated the press from censorship. Everyone was talking about the new *abertura,* or democratic opening up, that seemed in the offing. Many, though, were cynical about the prospects of real democracy returning so easily. Although official censorship had been lifted, there would continue to be heavy self-censorship from fear, and as Oscar Niemeyer warned, "the political situation could always worsen because they [the military] have the arms." And surfacing with the possibility of representation was the long-simmering discontent of the jobless and the grossly underpaid, who included most Brazilians. "Eighty percent of our money goes to the Army," complained a functionary of the district government whom I had found on his lunch hour reading an interview Fidel Castro had recently given to Brazilian journalist Fernando Morais.

Then, for my benefit, he read aloud a sentence of Fidel's: "I'm not sure Jimmy Carter comprehends that the most important problem with respect to human rights is the state of misery, hunger, malnutrition, and disease that millions and millions suffer in the underdeveloped world." One man who was optimistic about the *abertura* was Geisel's press secretary; he was as close as I would get to the aloof, enigmatic president, who didn't grant private interviews. "The revolution of 1964 was like the New Deal," said Colonel Ludwig. "It was necessary to put order in our house. Under Kubitschek there had been massive inflation. Then we entered a populist period that saw the spread of misery and anarchy. Now the rhythm of work and order has been established, the rights of habeas corpus have been restored, and we are entering a new political phase. Nineteen sixty-four to 1979 was an authoritarian period. Now the system will be more open." And Brasília, clearly, was booming. Real estate had skyrocketed. The trees planted in the *superquadras* were maturing, and the city no longer seemed so alien in the landscape, but to have been accommodated by it. So pleasant had life in the capital become, I was told, that congressmen from Rio and São Paulo, who only a few years before had bemoaned their exile in Brasília, were now refusing to vacate their government-provided apartments upon the expiration of their terms, and this was creating quite an apartment shortage. Brasília was now the Houston of Brazil, the most prosperous and fast-growing city in the country, but still too new to have found a recognizable identity.

Through all these political vicissitudes, the population of the Federal District had continued to grow prodigiously since the inauguration. The census of 1978 revealed the presence of 1,036,448 souls in the district, almost double the number in 1970. But only 264,180 of these inhabited the Plano itself; the other 74 percent dwelt in the eight satellite cities: Taguatinga, Nucleobandeirante (or "Pioneer Nucleus," as Cidade Livre had been renamed in 1961), Ceilândia, Gama, Guara, Sobradinho, Planaltina, and Brazlândia—with the exception of 26,420 souls classified as "rural," whose palm-thatch huts were scattered about the Federal District's 2,244 square miles. Eighty percent of the population to date had immigrated; 206,952 were native-born *candangos,* but for the last three years the migratory growth, which had fallen off since the early years to a mere 26,235, had been outstripped by the internal growth, with 31,747 births between 1976 and 1977. The migratory contingent, however, was still tremendously important, and it belonged to two main categories, the spontaneous and the induced, within which there were numerous currents and subsystems. Aldo Paviani, a geographer at the university and probably the foremost authority on the peopling of Brasília, identified five strains of migrant in a paper he co-authored in 1973. The first were those of higher status induced from the South. They knew what they were coming to, usually had firm job offers, and usually fared well, working in the Plano and living in a *superquadra.* The second were journeyman laborers and schoolteachers who came from the Northeast and earned the minimum wage, which in Brasília is about seventy-five dollars per month. The third, who made up about 25 percent of all migrants, were young construction workers from the neighboring states of Goiás, the unemployed, the jobless, and the illiterate, who had no skills and no income. And the last were the poor of similar status who came up from the South, particularly from São Paulo. All told, Paviani found that 64 percent were from the North, the Northeast, and the Center, and the remainder from the South and the Southeast. He also found that the size of the migration during a given year was highly dependent on the amount of construction that was going on in Brasília and on the situation at home, where flood and drought were the main fillips. "Not everybody comes here directly, either," Paviani told me in his office one afternoon. "Many go to several lesser cities before they get up the courage to come to Brasília. Feedback from previous immigrants—both negative and positive—is a tremendously important factor. In our model, propaganda about Brasília reaches the rural areas. The people there have a certain work capacity, aspirations, economic status, and age. They could migrate directly, but more often they come in stages, stopping a few years in City One, where they augment their aspirations and education, begin to want a higher salary, and are transformed into potentially successful migrants. From there they proceed to City Two or come directly to Brasília. If they can't make it here they either go back home or continue to São Paulo, where they presume they will find work. Many join the urban labor force that commutes daily from the *favelas* of São Paulo to the outlying fields of cotton, coffee, and sugarcane. This kind of person is being very exploited in São Paulo. He is called *bóia fria*, or 'cold grub,' because he takes his meals from a lunchbox. Urban migration is the most important demotic phenomenon in Brazil. In the last decade the rural population has only grown 6.7 percent while the urban population has increased by 65.3 percent. The attraction of the cities is that they have better work opportunities. But to survive in Brasília you must have some skill, or else go into construction, and you have to make at least the minimum wage."

One afternoon I went to see if I could find some of the people from whom Paviani had extrapolated his model. The real "marginals" don't arrive at the bus station; being able to buy a ticket already puts you in a more fortunate category. The *pau-de-araras* travel in the back of flatbed trucks and usually get out in Sobradinho because it is the first satellite city you come to as you approach the Federal District from the North; or in Taguatinga, because it is the largest of the satellite cities, with a population of 130,352 at the last census and enough industry of its own for half its labor force to find work within the city limits. There is a radio service in Taguatinga that helps new arrivals get in touch with their friends and relatives. "Pépé, your nephew is here," a typical broadcast might say. As in the Amazon and most of rural Brazil the material culture of the satellite cities is mainly pre-telephone, and the radio is the only way people can find each other and keep apprised of each other's movements. Because most of the marginals go directly to the houses of kin and friends, it is impossible to know how many slip into the city each day, but the number must be well over a hundred. Fifteen or so new marginals show up at the Nocturnal Hostelry of Sebastian the Martyr in Nucleobandeirante, a skidrow-type mission run by the popular spiritist sect with funds provided by the District. Here they get free meals, medical care, lodging, and advice on how to find a job. On the benches that lined the walls of the waiting room a dozen or so ragged and destitute people were sitting with their heads hung, neither moving nor talking. One man had come from the interior of São Paulo. He was clutching a bedroll on his lap and wore black shoes without socks or laces. His age was indeterminate, anywhere from thirty-five to sixty. All that remained to him was his pride. "Go away, I don't need reportage," he snapped when I started asking him questions. A woman from Pernambuco who was sitting on another bench amid nine of her eleven children was more willing to talk of her plight. "We came here because it was *ruim* [miserable] in Pernambuco. No work. We hitched rides and sometimes stopped to work. My husband is a truck driver and a mechanic. We were two months on the road. We started first in Sobradinho, then took care of a man's little weekend place in the country. That was nice, until the man sold it. It didn't work for us here. We went to the bus station and asked for passage to Pernambuco. A guard sent us here. I hope my husband can find a job so we can get the money to go home." She coaxed a pacifier into the mouth of her bawling baby. "This one has dysentary," she said, and directing her dull eyes across the room, "and that one over there has chickenpox." "Some come here thinking it's going to be easy," an attendant told me.

But marginals are not a significant group in the District, except that they are responsible for most of the still relatively low number of crimes that are committed. Only about a sixth end up staying; Brasília absorbs about six thousand of them a year. The vast majority who migrate integrate and are happy, as a 1966 survey of six hundred and fifty-three married men with stable residence in Brasília showed. Thirty-one percent of its subjects came from the South, 19 percent from the Southeast, 20 percent from the center, 29 percent from the North and Northeast. "Brasília represents a new, truly interregional Brazil," it concluded. Sixty-eight percent came with their families and were relatively young, with one of the highest fertility rates in Brazil. Their educational level was also relatively high: 11 percent had university degrees, 28 percent had completed high school, 23 percent were elementary school graduates, and 22 percent had started but not finished their elementary schooling, while 15 percent had never been to school at all. Twenty-six percent of the women worked outside of the house; Brasília was a land of opportunity for the career girl. Most of the people who directed themselves toward Brasília already had a migratory history (as Paviani would also find). Only 37 percent came straight from their homeland; the rest had previous migratory experience outside their state. Eighty percent had been to several cities before Brasília. Fifty-two percent said "lack of work opportunities at home" had driven them on. Eleven percent were transferred. Eleven percent said they couldn't resist the call of Brasília. Nine percent said the lack of institutional services at home had been a factor. Ten percent spoke of social problems like fights with relatives and a bad moral climate for their children. Twenty-five percent had trouble finding a job in the beginning. All complained of initial loneliness and anomie in the "lunar city" but 79 percent had managed to adapt and were planning to stay in the capital permanently. They praised the climate, the beauty of the city and its views, its pioneer spirit and its work opportunities.

None of the Leonias family was interviewed by Paviani, but they all conformed to the migratory pattern. The members came at different times and for different reasons, and some in a roundabout way. One evening in February happened to find most of them gathered at Iraci's house in Sobradinho. The occasion was Carnaval. The adults were drinking fiery *caipirinhas*, rum mixed with lemon and sugar, and watching the festivities in Rio on the television. But suddenly the power failed, as it does in Sobradinho with some frequency. Iraci produced some candles and everyone moved to the breezeway and sat around the long table watching them burn—Iraci and her grown children; Marie José; Waldemar and his wife, Terezinha; Marie de Lourdes and Isnard the cop; Luís Afonso and José Ademir; with Dona Joana at the head, puffing on a corncob pipe; and dozens of grandchildren screaming and tearing around the house. It began to rain, and very soon the pounding on the corrugated zinc roof became deafening, and through the chinks in the *comongó* we could see the water cascading off the edge of the roof and into the courtyard. The *comongó* is a feature of almost every Brazilian house, a wall with every other brick left out or, in another motif, butt-ends of red clay pipe stacked up in rows and cemented together. It ventilates the room that it helps enclose, enables the people inside to see what is going on outside without being easily detected, and unlike its American counterpart, the screen porch, is burglarproof. There was a *comongó* in the breezeway of the house in Floriano, and many an evening the family would sit there watching the carnaúba-wax candles burn on the table and the rain spattering into the courtyard, just as they were doing now. It wasn't hard to imagine, for a moment at least, that they had never left Piauí. One by one, each of them told the story of how he or she had come to be at this table and a resident of the

Federal District. As the senior male of the family and the first Leonias to establish himself in Brasília, Waldemar spoke first. Wiry and spry, with a high forehead, wavy black hair and mustache and grey chin stubble, he was forty-three now, a man of rare patience and physical stamina. One got the feeling he could go several days without nourishment and not be perturbed. As for drink, he could take it or leave it, but he preferred to take it. Wiping his hands across his mouth, he poured himself a shot of straight rum and belted it down. "We were all born in Piauí," he began. *"Clima tórrida."* He squeezed his cheeks to emphasize the sun's heat. "I worked in many places, but never got anything out of it except for helping a lot of people. Many of my friends are better off than I am. May God bring them happiness. I have no envy. I could have bought an apartment in the Plano years ago, but I was young and single and had everything I needed. In 1968 I went back to Piauí. They were stringing electric lines in Floriano. I met this good woman"—he stroked Terezinha—"woman, I've always said, is the mystery of life, the paradise of the eyes, and the purgatory of the purse." Universal laughter seconded the observation. "We have five children living. One died. Ocirene. But my work situation has always been a little precarious. I've never stopped at one place very long. Two months here, three months there. Looking back on it I can see that I didn't play my cards right. But there are two good things you can say about me. I respect others and have never stolen. There has never been a criminal in our family. You can go to whatever police station you please and you won't find a record on any one of us." Waldemar had been out of work for a few months. After Carnaval he was planning to start in as a supply clerk for a new subdivision that was going up in Sobradinho. At the beginning of the year he finally got his own house, one of 7007 units built in a low-income housing project called Guariroba, on the outskirts of Taguatinga. The house consisted of a bedroom, a living room, a bathroom, and a yard twenty-five by fifty-five feet. The terms were easy: no downpayment and twelve dollars a month, plus the light and water bills. "The houses are looked at as an investment for those who have nothing," Waldemar explained. "You can improve it—I've already planted a tangerine and a pitanga tree—or add a few rooms and sell it for something better. Some have already sold their houses for 40,000 cruzeiros (about $1,900 at the time). But if you sell you can never get another house from SHIS, the low-income housing authority. And if I die, my family gets to stay there for free." For several days before this reunion, Waldemar had been showing me the District. Having known Brasília when it was still empty, he was on a first-name basis with hundreds of its citizens, and a more knowledgeable guide couldn't have been asked for. He had taken me to Guariroba, whose houses were only a few feet apart and were each rigged with a tall, crooked pole to which a television aerial had been attached. Kites were already tangled in the light lines, and children swarmed in the raw spaces between rows. "With all the land still left in the District, why do we all have to live so close?" Waldemar complained. "But this will look a lot better when it is planted and painted and paved." I approached a group of children playing in several old truck tires. Though red dust coated their clothes and skin and the lower half of the white-washed wall behind them, their smiles were radiant.

Terezinha, or "Tété"—not Waldemar's wife, but his sister—was the next to come. She was thirty-four now, a bright, plump woman who had born five children. "I came here on December 26, 1963. I wanted to be a teacher and there were courses in education here that weren't offered in Piauí." Eventually she got a bachelor's degree in pedagogy and a job as a professor at a teacher's college in Sobradinho. In 1965—she was living with a family and paying room and board—she met her husband, Marco Aurelio de Lima, at a fair in which each Brazilian state had a tent. He was in the Ceará tent; his father is a well-known literary critic in Ceará. Marco had come with the idea of getting rich quickly and returning to his homeland. "But by the time you start making some money," he explained, "you're *desanimado* and getting older, so you end up staying." Marco was living with a cousin, and "my father sent me a little money so I could pay for my drinks, take the buses, and look for a job. I started out selling *carnets* door to door. *Carnets* are books of tickets that are redeemable for merchandise like cars and televisions, but you have to keep up with the payments. Then I entered the Bank of Brazil. Then I sold perfume for a while. Then I was part-owner of a clothing store. I've also owned at least half a dozen bars." For the last couple of years Marco had been back with the Bank of Brazil. Through the bank he'd been eligible for a nice house on a street in Sobradinho that was inhabited solely by colleagues in the bank, and he spent most of his Sundays rocking in a spacious green hammock under the carport, drinking Cuba libres and leafing through the *Correio Brasiliense*.

The de Lima children were striking. Carla Soraya, though only ten, was already shapely and very adult. Keila, eight, was pretty enough to be a child model, while Fernanda, with her straight black hair and darker pigmentation, looked like an Indian. More than any of the Leonias clan in Brasília, Tété's family had achieved a comfortable middle-class existence.

Nita, as everyone called Maria de Lourdes, was the next to come. As a teenager she'd been cheeky and beautiful. "I was working in a store that sold animal skins. One of the partners wanted to *enamorar* with me. I didn't. He stole millions of cruzeiros and I was blamed because I was the cashier. I was sacked but not prosecuted. A few months later the partner started showing up with expensive clothes and a new car, and it was obvious who had done it. But I was never fully vindicated and the people in Floriano ate up the scandal. There were many, I think, who resented my beauty." Not long afterward, Nita developed a mysterious goiter on her neck that swelled up until it was as large as a grapefruit. No doctor in Floriano could diagnose it. She went to Fortaleza, a large city on the coast, but the doctors there felt it was hopeless and refused to operate. Finally, in 1964, she came to Brasília, where at last she found a surgeon who diagnosed the goiter as a thyroid condition and removed it. After forty-two days in the hospital she was released, and she began a new life. "All this had happened to me, and I was only eighteen. I took a course with the telephone company, but ended up a manicurist. I go from house to house, on foot mostly, carrying my materials. I spend an hour and a half to two hours per manicure and get eighty cruzeiros if it is in Gama, where I live, and a hundred and twenty if I have to go to the Plano. First I clean the nails with polish remover. Then I pare the cuticles with a small pair of scissors and file them down with a piece of orangewood; if they want their feet done, too, I use a pumice stone. Then I apply the base, and after it has dried, the polish itself, scintillant or lactant, depending on the customer's preference. Some day I'd like to set up a beauty parlor in my own house. I've already got the chair. All I need is a big mirror and a dryer." For the last six years Nita had been living in a rented *barraca* with Isnard, a traffic policeman. Their application for a house in a fifteen-thousand-unit project being constructed near Guariroba had been accepted, and they were just waiting to hear when they could move in. When Nita went out to work, their two infant children were looked after by Samara, eight, Nita's child from a previous relationship.

Tadeu, who came down in 1965, was absent. An active thirty-one-year-old bachelor, he had served for many years in the Military Police, and after finally making sergeant and getting a little seniority, he had abruptly left the force a few months ago. "I think he got tired of being a tough guy," one of his sisters conjectured. Now he was working as a dispatcher for SHIS, helping people who had qualified for low-income housing assemble the interminable documents they would need before they could take possession of their house. In a few weeks he would quit that to become a bus driver for the Pioneer Line between Taguatinga and the Plano. I'd met Tadeu a couple of times. He was always well-dressed, with becoming mustaches and sideburns, and always seemed to gravitate to the prettiest woman in the vicinity. But he hardly ever came around to Sobradinho, and of all the Leonias family I knew him least.

In 1968 Ana, Iraci's child, decided to see what Brasília was all about. She came alone; spunkiness was a quality she had never lacked. She was only twelve and lived with Marco and Tété. In June of the following year, Iraci herself came, and she was followed by her son Paulo a month later. Ana took me to their first house in the Federal District, a precarious free-form *barraca* that was still standing, to her amazement, around the corner from the house in which Marco was stabbed. There were two rooms. To take a shower, there was a pipe in one of the walls that you squatted under. Once while showering Ana looked up and discovered that two boys had climbed the avocado tree and were watching her through a gap in the roof. With twenty years of teaching experience, Iraci found a job before the month was out. Soon they were joined by Waldemar. His daughter had just died of dehydration in Piauí, and the work there had run out. He was hired on as *apontador* at the Santa Maria dam, which by December 1979 held a reservoir of twenty-one billion gallons and was supplying Brasília with most of its water. Ana grew bored with life in Gama. It was an hour and a half from the Plano, and there was little for her to do after school except to go down with her friends to the waterfall that plunged into a nearby gorge. Because her grades were good, she was transferred to one of the better schools in the Plano, where she met the children of government ministers and congressmen and became aware that there was a privileged class. In 1970 she watched television for the first time in the house of Tété's neighbor, and thought it quite marvelous. By hard work Iraci enabled her family to rent a succession of houses, each a little nicer than the last, and in 1972, by a stroke of good luck, a charming little cottage prefabricated in São Paulo and assembled on a lush, quiet street in Sobradinho, became available when the original buyer backed out, and Iraci grabbed it. Sobradinho was only half an hour from the Plano, an easy commute for Ana, who bought a used car on the installment plan, took driving lessons, and by eighteen had her license. At night she took courses at the Cultur Inglês; every good-sized city in Brazil has at least one such institution devoted to the study of English, and they are very popular, particularly with the young. Ana's teacher, however, was a Brazilian who had learned *her* English from a Brazilian, so by the time it was transmitted to her, it bore little resemblance to the language that is heard in the various English-speaking parts of the world. At five feet ten, Ana was exceptionally tall and a natural athlete. She played volleyball and basketball well and excelled at handball, not the game known by that name here, but a cross between basketball and soccer, invented in Germany, in which the teammates dribble and pass their way down a short court and try to throw the ball, which is about three-fourths the size of a soccer ball, past a goal keeper and into a goal that is about half the size of a soccer goal. A fast-paced game, fun to play and watch, it is wildly popular in Brazil. After graduating from high school with a degree in elementary schoolteaching, she tried to get into the university. The competition for the eight hundred places in the freshman class was very stiff and so was the entrance exam, called the *vestibular,* equivalent to the French *baccalauréat* and the English A-levels. Ana took the *vestibular* three times, in biology, communications, and law, but each time there were eight hundred applicants with a higher score. So she took a course in *biblioteconomia,* in which she learned the techniques of microfilming and filing books and got a job in the university's vast library.

By now she had left her gangly teens and ripened into a stunning *mulata* like the women who are the subject of most Brazilian love songs. The three races of Brazil had blended in her in a most felicitous way. She had the stately height and the full mouth of an African, the fine nose and eyebrows of a Portuguese, the high cheekbones of an Indian. Swarms of suitors—medical students, engineers, and other young professionals—buzzed around her. She took *concursos*, tests which were also fiercely competitive, for positions in the State Department, the Federal Police, and the National Indian Foundation. In 1975 she joined the latter. I met her there in the fall of 1976, and we were married the following spring.

Tall Paulo, with his manly self-assurance and features that recalled the young Frank Sinatra, had already left, at twenty-four, a trail of brokenhearted women in his wake. He was still studying, always buried in a textbook, biding his time before entering the working adult world. He lived with his mother as almost all Brazilian men do until they marry, and a new gentleness and protectiveness could be noticed in his attitude toward her since Ana had left the house; with his sister in the States, he was all she had now. Paulo received a small monthly scholarship of nine hundred cruzeiros from the District, and in two years he would have two degrees, one in mathematics and one in physics, with which he hoped to enter the growing computer field, or failing that, to teach. He was also studying, along with thirteen thousand others, for a *concurso* that would be given in the Emilio Médici Sports Arena for eight hundred coveted positions in the Regional Bank. He had had to wait in line for eight hours just to register. "In Brazil," he explained, "getting a job doesn't depend on whom you know, but on the outcome of your *concurso,* and once you get the job, it's practically impossible to be fired." His attitude toward the *concurso* was relaxed, because he felt it was a long shot. In the evenings he stepped out with his pretty girlfriend

Sonja, who worked at Sears Roebuck, one of the largest department stores in the Plano. With his two avuncular contemporaries, Lulu and Budim, he played soccer in the pickup game that would materialize Sunday mornings in the field below Iraci's house; in 1977 I helped plant the lichen-encrusted goalposts, cut in a nearby gallery forest. It was a very serious game. Reputations were at stake. The average barefoot urchin in Brazil can dribble circles around the best players in the Ivy League. Practically every nuance of the game has a name. A goal that ricochets off a side post is *paulista;* if it glances off the top bar, it is a *carioca,* the most esteemed kind of goal. I watched Paulo make a *carioca.* Picking himself up from the ground after his valiant vain leap, the goalie muttered, "In a game like this, it's hard for the goalie. If they shoot hard, it goes in."

Of all the family, Iraci's life was probably the least affected by the move from Floriano. She continued to teach a double shift, leaving the house at seven and returning at six that evening, as she had always done. Upon rising she ate a plateful of rice and beans with a sprinkling of *farinha,* or manioc meal, kneading and scooping it up with her fingers, and then nothing except perhaps an orange until evening, when she ate rice and beans again, often with meat and a sliced tomato. Our attempts to introduce interesting new items to her diet like cucumbers or mushrooms met with stern resistance. "I've eaten this food all my life and have the health of an ox," she would argue, and it was true. At forty-seven she had never been seriously ill and was remarkably robust, with the same auburn hair that years ago had caught the attention of João Paulo dos Santos, and only a suggestion of grey at her temples. Her life was solitary, the evening and weekends spent putting the house in order, visiting with Tété's family, or watching television. She had no telephone and couldn't justify the expense of one. "I don't call anyone, and nobody calls me." Iraci was a deeply religious woman. She would always kiss us on both cheeks and say, *"Vai com Deus e Nossa Senhora,"* whenever we were leaving the house, even if it was only to walk uphill to the bakery. She was also quite superstitious. If a knife fell to the floor, she would say, "A man is coming" (a spoon would have meant the arrival of a woman). She knew dozens of folk remedies that she administered to her children and herself with positive results. Tea made from the grated avocado pit was a diuretic; avocado-leaf tea calmed the intestines. Orange-peel tea with a lot of sugar put a quick stop to the meanest cold. And her penmanship was the finest I have ever seen.

Antonio Hedevirgem, or Tonho, wasn't at the gathering either, because his second child was due at any moment. Thirty now, he'd been driving buses since coming down to Brasília in 1974. Then, two months ago, he'd decided he needed a rest. "What with the overcrowding and the deafening motor, whose muffler is often rusted out, right under the driver's seat, and people pulling the cord every two seconds, I was becoming *doidinho, nervoso, agonhado,*" he explained, "a complete basket case." Besides, he and Iraçema, his old lady, were very much in love, and he wanted to be with her when the baby came. Marco had just sold him a color television set so they were spending most of their time in front of it, waiting. Later that week, Christiane was born. In a few weeks Tonho's savings would run out, and he'd have to report again at the bus yard. He hadn't realized that after two years with his niece I could speak fairly good Portuguese, and he still communicated with me half in sign language. His main expression was *quente,* literally "hot" but closer to the "cool" of our slang, accompanied by the thumbs-up sign. When we had met again for the first time in two years he asked me to play "The House of the Rising Sun" on the guitar, and as I was playing it, he began to cry. "I can't help it," he sobbed. "Whenever I hear that song, it reminds me of you."

Marie José, or "Bibi," came down in September 1974. Like

Tété and Iraci, she was a teacher and had started her career in Piauí in a remote village called Ribeirão Gonçalves, which was accessible only by jeep and boat. "I married the mayor's son," she said. "There were three children from this union, but our spirits never combined. We never fought, but one day, since neither of us was making the other happy, we just decided to separate. I don't know where he is now. He sent us a postcard from the Amazon a few years ago, but that's the last anyone's heard of him. I returned to Floriano and worked my way up to principal of one of the best elementary schools in the city. But after the 1974 elections the new mayor appointed his nephew principal of the school—that's how the system works in Piauí—and I was out of a job. So I came to see Tété. Though I told her I was just on vacation, she made me take a *concurso* for a principal's position in Ceilândia, and I was offered the job. The pay was five times what I'd been making in Piauí (though still less than three hundred dollars a month)." Ceilândia, the grimmest and most squalid of the satellite cities, was created in 1970. Its name means "The land of the campaign to eradicate the invasions." In less than two months, more than eighty thousand squatters were moved to it from four large "invasions" where the haphazard spread of shanties had reached *favela* proportions. The squatters were given lots to homestead and allowed to put up *barracas* provided that within a certain period they were replaced with more substantial brick-and-mortar structures. Light, sewage, and water were promised, but to this day they are inadequate in much of the city, which is still mostly *barracas,* with few trees, no paved roads, a dusty, depressed landscape. Crime and ignorance are higher in Ceilândia than anywhere in the District because a high percentage of the population is destitute. *Macumba* is widespread. One night Bibi took me to a *macumba* session. We sat gripping the railing in the gallery of the small, board-and-batten meeting house, the men on one side, women on the other, as a half-dozen large black women in bandanas and long white skirts, puffing cigars and pulling at bottles of rum, reeled and spun about the room, shuddering violently, rolling their eyes, emitting excited little yips, babbling incoherently, and sometimes fainting outright as each was possessed by her respective spirit; and all the while a battery of men beating congo drums, cymbals, tambourines, and other percussion instruments kept up a steady, intoxicating rhythm. Having just come from eight months among aboriginal Indians, I wasn't impressed; it lacked the depth and sincerity of a real primitive ceremony; the truly entranced don't keep casting furtive glances to the gallery. Bibi accepted her less than optimal new life with her usual good cheer; she is an imperturbable person, one of whose endearing traits is a tendency to break into song at the slightest provocation. "I went through a lot of culture shock at the beginning," she confessed. "The climate here was colder, it was a long commute to the school and back, and there was all this talk about robberies and assaults. I had always been used to leaving the door of my house open. I had never known this fear. After six months I was ready to leave, but I stayed, because it is better for my children here." Until a few months before Bibi and her three daughters had rented a comfortable blue-painted *barraca* in Ceilândia from a man who was building a cinderblock house in front of the lot. But when the house was finished the man had been obliged by law to tear down the *barraca,* and Bibi had moved to Guariroba, a few miles away. She was much happier in the new project, and her house was only a few rows from Waldemar's. Vita, her oldest, eighteen, had already entered sultry womanhood. She had missed the 1978 school year when a neighbor hit her with his car as she was waiting at the bus stop, shattering her right tibia and forcing her to spend fourteen months in a cast. Livia was a buxom fifteen-year-old, and freckled Valeria was in Rio, staying with her uncle Francisco and having some work done on her teeth.

Dona Joana's last two children, Budim (José Ademir) and

Lulu (Luís Afonso), stayed with her for a few months after her husband's death in November 1974, until she could settle her affairs, then all three came down to the capital. Both were still in her care, which meant that they were in fact being supported by their brother Francisco, who was his mother's legal guardian. But Lulu had been on his own for a year, driving trucks. Though he was a licensed teamster, the profession is not organized and not the well-paid brotherhood that it is in the United States, and Lulu was lucky to take home a hundred and fifty dollars a month. He was twenty-three, with a bush of kinky black hair, lean and catlike and exuberantly alive. He seemed in perpetual motion, on the very edge of nervous control, always about to upset the external order around him. He had been living off and on with a pretty seventeen-year-old from São Paulo. She'd had a child, "but it wasn't mine. It was *suspeito*." "No traces of the family," the family had agreed. He'd driven trucks to Belo Horizonte, Rio, Petrópolis, Teresópolis, and back; he hauled turf, cement, lumber, furniture. He'd worked two months for Dona Joana's brother Manoel, who had a ranch in the Amazon with nine hundred head of zebu cattle, and shipped the native hardwoods: mahogany, Jenny wood, peppertree. He'd driven a truck for Mesbla, the Gimbel's of Rio, and delivered purchases to customers in every *bairro* in the city. Now he was thinking of trying out São Paulo.

Budim, three years Lulu's senior, was an *auxiliar de contabilidade*. He telephoned people who owed money and got a percentage of whatever he persuaded them to pay up.

These, then, were the Leonias family of Brasília, late of Floriano, Piauí, my in-laws. In many respects they were typical not only of the people who had come to inhabit the satellite cities of the capital, but of the majority of Brazilians. By most definitions they belonged to the lower middle class. The cutoff point between *classe pobre* and *classe média* accepted by most Brazilian sociologists is an income of double the minimum wage,

91

although some require the subject to earn three *salários minimos*. According to another definition, whether or not one has a car, only Tété's and Iraci's households and Francisco would qualify for the middle class, though Tonho and Tadeu have also owned cars at various times. "Having a car creates a different mentality," a sociologist explained. "It is already a symptom that you are trying to better yourself." As for telephones, only Tété's household had one. The telephone was not a crucial accessory in any of their lives, because their pattern of socializing was spontaneous. No one called ahead to agree on a mutually satisfactory time to visit; they just dropped in. The Leonias family was very tight, their own best friends and confidants. They got together often and socialized almost exclusively among themselves. The clan was large enough to offer a spectrum of personalities, and something new and interesting was always happening to one of them. In Brazil the family is the fortress, the main unit of order and stability in a world that is periodically plunged into political and economic chaos and subject to recurrent natural disaster. Communities like the ones that evolved in New England, with their strong democratic tradition of the townspeople meeting and deciding on matters of common concern, are unknown in Brazil, though communications among Brazilian neighbors are, paradoxically, far more warm and extensive than they are in the temperate world. They are not so much communities as groups of friendly independent families. Each house, each family plot, is heavily fortified, as they were in Iberia, with unscalable outer walls, often tipped with broken glass, screening off the garden and courtyard, bars on all the windows, locks on all the outer doors, and often a mangy, emaciated dog who has attached himself to the household in return for the bones and leftovers and will bark his head off at any interloper. Each family stands against the world.

I first glimpsed the futuristic mirage of Brasília on the evening of September 14, 1976, from a window of the Transbrasíliana, the bus that runs from Belém to the capital. I had gotten on the bus thirty-six hours before, and as the bus entered the tedious series of concentric rings which eventually delivered it, like water swirling down a drain, to the bus station, I blearily reminded myself to check at the earliest opportunity whether water in the Southern Hemisphere swirls down drains in a counterclockwise fashion, as, by dint of the Coriolis force, it is supposed to. I had been in Brazil just a week. The Sierra Club had asked me to write a book about the Amazon, and I had jumped at the opportunity; for someone with an interest in natural history the Amazon was perhaps the ultimate place to visit, and I wanted to get there while I was still young and unattached, because the chance to spend eight months roaming in the jungle would probably not come so easily later. But before I could leave civilization I had to get a permit from the National Indian Foundation in Brasília. Getting a permit wouldn't be easy, a British anthropologist who'd been kept waiting six months told me. "Make your application as academic-sounding as possible," had been his advice. And so, in a document that was translated into Portuguese by a girl at the American Embassy, I emphasized the ethnobotanical part of it. No one had collected and catalogued the medicinal plants in the Cayapo Indian village of Mekranoti; this I would do. To cultivate a more scholarly appearance I wore a droopy blue bowtie with white polkadots and the same baggy old seersucker suit in which I'd successfully dealt with government officials in Tallahassee, Florida, four years earlier. The girls at FUNAI, as the Indian Foundation is called, could scarcely control their amusement at my outfit. They accepted my application and told me there was nothing to do but wait. I waited a month. Soon they had a nickname for me: *barboleta,* or butterfly, a reference to the bowtie.

For most of the month I read up on Indians in the library at

FUNAI. The foundation took up most of a thirteen-story building in the Southern Commercial Sector, a dense stand of high-rise structures whose height and close proximity to each other are not typical of the city. It was a small, poorly ventilated room with an impressive collection of anthropological material, mostly about the Amazon. One afternoon, as I was close to nodding off with a soporific doctoral thesis in my lap, a nearby female voice, speaking Portuguese, brought me to life. I looked up to find a tall, shapely young woman, with high cheekbones and skin like golden silk, standing in front of me. Having no idea what she was saying (the question was, I would later learn, "Are you Marcos?"), I gave her a helpless little shrug. She smiled and left the room. Who was that, I wondered, and what had she wanted? In a little while she returned with two demitasses of sweet black coffee, sat beside me, and started trying out her English. I produced my two-way Collier's pocket dictionary in its pebbly green jacket, and in the next hour we must have passed that little volume back and forth a hundred times.

Her name was Ana dos Santos, and she was a typist who worked in the adjoining room, where telegrams were radioed to FUNAI's one hundred and seventy-two field stations. I asked how she liked working with the Indians. They were good people, she said, but *un pouco exigentes*—always asking for things. It was almost quitting time before I got up the courage to ask her to dinner. She said she was having some trouble with her car and would have to think about it. Then she went back to her typewriter, but as everyone was leaving the building she came back to the library and said, "Okay. *Vamos.*"

Continuing our spirited attempts at communication, we went down some stairs that led from the Southern Commercial Sector to the Sector of Diversions, on one of the well-worn footpaths which the citizens had established in defiance of the more circuitous sidewalks they were supposed to use. Distances in

Brasília, on foot or by car, are long, and deviations from both the pedestrian and the highway plans are numerous. We were a couple of hundred yards south of where the South Wing of the airplane-shaped Pilot Plan joins the fuselage. I was still getting used to all the glass. We had gone outside just in time to see the sinking sun color every west-facing windowpane. With Ana on my arm, I was beginning to feel better about Brasília. No city in my experience, I had to confess, was so open to the sky. Brasília had none of the darkness and dinginess of older cities, and none of the odor of fear. Lacking heavy industry, it had no pollution, either, and except for the paperclips that littered the sidewalks—some bureaucratic fallout was inevitable—it was spotlessly clean. Most important, the people seemed warm, happy, and well-adjusted, and to be suffering no ill effects from the relentlessly rectilinear architecture.

The largest building in the Sector of Diversions, where we had dinner, is called the Conjunto Nacional, and it was, at the time of its opening in 1973, the largest commercial complex in South America. Four stories high, with two more below ground, it had a façade of varicolored vertical neon signs, all pulsing at different intervals; it is a bedizened building in the best Brazilian tradition. That such a tradition existed even before the arrival of neon lighting I learned from a book by John Foster Fraser, an Englishman who, passing through Pernambuco in 1913, described its central avenue as "a wide main thoroughfare with bedizened buildings on either side." The interior of the building was shared by a bewildering array of concerns whose juxtaposition suggested the discernible scheme: strobelit *pimbol* parlors patronized by young Army recruits in green fatigues with the sides of their heads shaven (every Brazilian male without a good excuse is required to do a year of military service); soft-porn movie theaters (only breasts may be bared on the Brazilian screen, and the naked starlets have to keep crossing their legs deftly so that nothing else is revealed); record

95

stores and sunglass stores; stores devoted to the sale of framed prints; stores filled with Brasília bric-a-brac—postcards, miniature wooden replicas of the *Two Candangos* statue, lacquered ashtrays with scenes of the Monumental Sector. In the midst of this Forty-second Street glitter were more sophisticated boutiques with expensive clothing from abroad; suits by Pierre Cardin and Ted Lapidus of Paris; shirts and ties by Christian Dior and Yves Saint-Laurent. Since their main patrons were the irresponsible offspring of ministers and diplomats who seldom followed up after the first downpayment, the average life expectancy of these boutiques was short, about six months. In fact, almost every concern in the Conjunto Nacional except for the stalwart Sears Roebuck, the bank branches, and the offices of lesser Latin American countries too poor to afford an embassy on the Avenida das Nações, seemed to be threatened with *liquidação total, hiperliquidação,* and even, in the case of one window sign, *demolição* of its entire stock. On the bottom floor was a large supermarket and a discount furniture store whose ceiling was strung with pennants on which a cartoon figure who looked like Donald Duck but wore a Superman costume was saying (in Portuguese, of course):

> For those in a hurry who want it now; for those who want time to pay.

Since the bulk of Brasília's work force are low-salaried employees of the government, everyone buys on time. Credit is easy to get because it's often the only way a merchant can move his goods, and most of the customers are a good risk because they stay at their jobs and need a good credit reference. As long as your record with the Departamento de Proteção Credito is clean, you can keep going; if not, you're finished. A cousin of the Leonias family, married to a sensationally attractive woman with expensive tastes who also happened to be a cousin, had run into trouble by overextending himself shortly before I arrived in Brasília. His wife had insisted on a weekend house in the country besides their apartment in Cruzeiro, on a new car plus various appliances, a large clothing allowance, and their children's enrollment in the Alliance Francaise. Early one morning, after he had been missing for twenty-four hours, his colleagues at the bank had found him wandering around in a vacant lot and talking distractedly to himself. "What am I going to do? I'm ruined." Taking up a collection, his friends at work had raised the five thousand dollars he needed.

Ana and I dined gluttonously for less than four dollars apiece at a barbecue restaurant on the third floor. Waiters who walked from table to table with flashing knives and various cuts of beef, pork, chicken, and sausage on long spits, sliced off as much as we could eat. The waiters outnumbered the customers by two to one, since besides us there was only a beet-red blond male tourist and a black girl with a two-foot-wide platinum Afro wig. Music was provided by a singer who (our waiter told us proudly) had come "all the way from Rio," and playing the Moog synthesizer furnished his own rhythm section, piano, and bass. After dinner, we shopped for a movie. Rejecting *Brilhantina,* the Portuguese-dubbed version of *Grease,* we settled on a Brazilian work that had been panned in that morning's *Correio Brasiliense* as "a ridiculous film which compromises careers and condemns the director to eternal hellfire." What it was about I no longer remember; we sat in the back row and Ana joked about how the armrest was an *obstáculo.* A group of youths jeered and whistled throughout the performance, ruining it, such as it was, for the rest of us, and when it let out Ana told me they were *playboys,* the local term for the spoiled, idle progeny of Brasília's well-to-do, who have little to do for kicks except to hang out at the Conjunto Nacional, smoke marijuana smuggled in from Paraguay, and bomb around in sports cars.

Ana explained that she lived in the suburbs with her mother

97

and would have to go home now. We walked over to the bus station and descended an escalator. A man was trying to coax a frightened woman from the hinterland, evidently on her first visit to the capital, to get on it, too, but she wouldn't budge and they ended up taking the regular stairs. On the lower level there were long lines before signs bearing the names of the satellite cities. The people in the lines were noticeably darker-skinned than the ones I had been meeting; were one's experience of Brazil solely the Pilot Plan of the capital, one could be misled into thinking that it was a country of light-skinned people. The lines had shortened considerably since rush hour, when, between the erratic schedules of the buses and the number of people waiting to get on them, it usually takes an hour before it is possible to board. The Brazilian queuing system is quite different from the British one: when a bus finally arrives, the patient line suddenly dissolves and there is a mad rush for the door, and in the gleeful free-for-all, the ones who shove the hardest get on. The Brazilians are a physically gregarious people; in their paintings, the landscape is always packed with people, and one notices, too, at the crowds that pack the soccer stadiums (I was once bodily lifted off the ground and carried along for several feet in the swell of a soccer crowd), that everyone is laughing. Once the bus is chock-full, which means that a few people must be only halfway in and hanging on for dear life, it throws up a thick screen of diesel smoke and pulls out, and gathering momentum in the rings around the station, finally lurches off toward its destination.

Ana and I saw a lot of each other, and after several weeks I asked if I could meet her mother. That evening—a Friday—we set out in her Variant, a sturdy stationwagon put out by Volkswagen of Brazil, on the road for Sobradinho. A proverb was taped to the dashboard: *A inveja é a incapacidade própria.* Envy is pure incapacity. Within five minutes we had left the city and entered the stark savanna that comes right up to its edge and surrounds it for as far as the eye can see—a ten-mile-wide greenbelt that has been set aside in perpetuity, and is one of the capital's best features. Few signs of human activity were visible in it: a *casebra,* or mud-and-wattle hovel that probably predated the city, and wading toward it through the tall grass, a bent old woman hauling a load of faggots with a tumpline; the grove of centenarian mango trees on the old Fazenda Torto, some with five-foot diameters and probably the biggest trees in the District; a roadside stand of watermelons, which were introduced to Brazil by a handful of Confederates who fled there after the disappointing outcome of the Civil War; a speed trap set up by the highway police (it is forbidden to exceed fifty miles per hour, but if you are caught, a hundred-cruzeiro note slipped into the breast pocket of the understanding officer will usually get you "liberated"); piles of debris from construction sites dumped outside the city limits; *imprestos,* fill cuts with thin ridges of the original hillside left to prove how much earth had been excavated. It was two long rises and two long dips to Sobradinho. Two boys on bicycles were hanging to a truck lumbering up the first grade. On the second there had been an accident. A bus had gone off the road and rolled down into a gully. Dozens of cars had pulled over and their occupants had run to the edge of the gully to see what had happened. "No one admires anything quite so much as a really gruesome automobile accident," John Gunther wrote of the Brazilians in 1940. The second dip was under repair; three years later, when I revisited Sobradinho, it would still be under repair. The little houses of Sobradinho smothered the hillside to the left. Five thousand two hundred of them were counted in a 1969 census; today there must be twice as many. Most of them, like Tété's and Iraci's, are *casas populars,* brightly painted stucco-over-cinderblock structures with flat tops or sloping tile roofs. A few hundred are fancier *caixotes,* "crates," literally. Covered with hand-painted tiles—the handsomest have a blue rosette on each

99

square—with grated windows and doors, and sliding metal bars to protect their carports, they look like gaudy pillboxes. A few two-story mansions rivaling those on Lake Paranoá have recently appeared on one street, and there are a good number of well-made *barracas*. The women of Sobradinho take great pride in their gardens, Ana told me, and each year there is a competition for the best one. Showy-flowering trees—African tulip, flame tree, yellow cassia, lavender jacaranda—line the streets, and in the yards banana, avocado, mango, citrus, cashew, and papaya trees drip with fruit. The papayas are not picked until they have reached the size of cantaloupes. The puny little papayas that occasionally make their way into North American supermarkets are called *pecados;* no one in Sobradinho would deign to eat these "transgressions." Sobradinho post-dates the Plano by only a few months. It started block by block in the summer of 1960 as various organs of the government constructed tasteful housing for their employees. Strangely enough, there are no *sobrados* in Sobradinho. Years ago there was only a ranch called Fazenda Sobradinho because an ovenbird had built a two-story mud-daubed nest on an arm of a wooden cross that overlooked the property. Most ovenbird nests are two-story affairs, and because the bird sang beautifully at dusk and had chosen such a holy site, the whole business was regarded by a group of hands at the *fazenda* as a small miracle. Auguste de St. Hilaire, a French naturalist who made pioneer botanical collections in central and southern Brazil, spent a night at Fazenda Sobradinho in June 1819. "I was told I would see a lot of wildlife, but saw none," he complained to his notebook. "The time of insect proliferation had passed. There were few butterflies and very few plants were in flower. I was impressed with the immense solitude of the region. The population of all Goiás is sixty thousand, including slaves but not Indians; and of these but ten thousand are white. Toward dark, as I approached Fazenda Sobradinho, I thought I saw a rhea and a wildcat in the distance. The *fazenda* was on the edge of a forest through which a clear stream ran. A white woman, still young and pretty, received me and let me stay the night. Instead of hiding, as most of the women do when they see a stranger, she stayed and conversed. She seemed happy with the life she had, commenting indignantly that a previous traveler had told her that the isolation of these backlands was terrible. She knew nothing of the world except her home and her domestic routine so how could she not but love them? The night was very cold. The next day was hot, and I discovered a stand of dwarf bamboos like the ones at Paranoá that still don't have a name." Years later, as Red, the valley site, Sobradinho would almost be chosen for the capital, but instead it would become the calmest and the choicest of the satellite cities.

It was already dark by the time we descended the deeply eroded red dirt lane to Iraci's house, activating the barks of numerous dogs. We passed some children filling plastic bags with huge black June bugs that had hatched by the thousands in the moonlight, and a stand of red candles that *macumba* cultists had left at a streetcorner as an offering to the spirits. Iraci's house was pink, with a tall television aerial, the second one from the end on the last street at the bottom of the hill. A cement path led to the door through a lovingly tended garden with shapely rosebushes, philodendrons, dense mats of zoysia grass, impatiens (which the Brazilians call Maria-without-shame because it spreads everywhere), and a white-and-purple flowering shrub known as good day and good night. Inside Iraci's house, her sister Nita, and Armando, a truckdriver who dropped in sometimes in the evening, were engrossed in a television soap opera called "Checkmate." We struggled gamely to converse for several hours and I ended up spending the night on the sofa. Somewhere after midnight Paulo returned with red dirt on his

101

cream-colored dancing shoes, folded out a cot, and stretched out beside me. In the morning I opened the back door and looked out. Iraci's white rabbit and the neighbor's cat were sleeping together on an old oil drum beneath the tattered, gently fluttering banana tree, and in the distant meadow some naked boys were stalking birds with slingshots. The street in front of the house had already come to life. I could hear the banana man, who was already pushing his wheelbarrow full of fruit, calling lustily to the housewives, "Here comes the banana man. Come and get your bananas, cheap and good." He was followed by a man with a grinding wheel over his shoulder who would blow a scale on a plastic panpipe and sing out: "Here comes the knife-sharpener. Any dull knives or scissors, ladies? Bring them here and I will sharpen them." The children were already playing in the street, where they would remain for the better part of the day. The girls were skipping rope, the boys expertly shooting marbles or chasing after hoops. A white mule with blinds over its eyes pulled a wooden cart that had automobile wheels with tires, and a boy, proudly conscious of his responsibility, stood on the seat and held the reins. Two heavily madeup Jehovah's Witness girls knocked at Iraci's door and tried to interest her in a publication called *Awake*.

My permit came through in record time—two weeks—and it would take another fortnight for the young Belgian anthropologist who would accompany me to Mekranoti to get his papers in order. Soon there would be nothing to keep me in Brasília, except Ana. By this time we were even using the word "love," and the thought of being severed from her—forever, unless I changed my itinerary—was unbearable. I was charmed by her relaxed sweetness, by the cleanness of her soul, by the way she pared an orange so that the skin fell to the floor in a long coil, and a hundred other things. So I asked her to marry me. She agreed, after some insistence, as long as we didn't live in America forever and she could make frequent trips to visit her mother. Ana and Iraci were very close. They even, for want of space, shared the same bed. Her daughter was Iraci's chief consolation in a life that had been mostly disappointing, and every month they would join their paychecks and concoct the devious strategies that Brazilians who are not well off devise to weather the inflation. So I did not fully realize what I was asking when, one night at a restaurant in Sobradinho, I asked Iraci for her daughter's hand. Iraci stiffened when she understood the question, then nodded and looked down gravely at her hands. For a long time she said nothing, but stared at the wedding band that she still wore and twisted it back and forth anxiously around her finger. At length she turned to Ana and asked her if she wanted the marriage, and Ana, smiling through watering eyes, nodded yes. Then Iraci heaved a great sigh and said, "My daughter means everything to me. I will give you my answer tomorrow."

The next morning we drove to visit Nita in Gama and as we cruised between rows of eucalyptus trees, the sunlight flickered in their branches and I tried to strengthen my case. My main argument was that I could give Ana a better life in America. Iraci listened carefully, nodding slowly from time to time. She seemed impressed. Periodically Ana would lean over and give me a kiss of encouragement.

Nita's *barraca* had a cement floor and a corrugated zinc roof, and it was sided with weathered grey planks. The family lived in three sparsely furnished rooms, sharing the front porch and yard with another family who lived in a separate wing. On a peg in the front room was Isnard's white police cap, with a flap that descended around the back and side like the helmet of the Foreign Legion. A record of rural accordion music from the Northeast was turning on a small, battery-powered Victrola.

Enticing smells were coming from the kitchen: Dona Joana was baking tapioca cakes. She took my hand gently and told me that she herself had married at fourteen and had fourteen children and twenty-eight grandchildren to date. Ana, the second-oldest grandchild, would be the first of her generation to marry. Around lunchtime the rest of the family descended in a three-car caravan. It was a regular *invasão* of relatives, as Nita put it. The whole clan was there. Even Lulu, a happy-go-lucky nineteen-year-old, and Francisco, a more serious, bearded thirty-two-year-old who had a good position at the Bank of Brazil and was a year from getting his degree in industrial psychology, happened to have come up from Rio. Everyone was naturally interested in meeting the suitor of their favorite niece, and everyone had his opinion about whether or not the marriage should take place. Several things about me were not in my favor, the main ones being that I was divorced, not a Catholic and just passing through. My profession was neither acceptable nor comprehensible: who had ever heard of anyone making a living out of writing, especially when the writing was about animals and plants? Marco Aurelio's father was a well-known literary critic, but even he worked in a bank to support himself. Maybe—I caught a few furtive looks being cast at my medium-length hair—I was one of those hippies. The two of us sat in the kitchen holding hands and talking with Dona Joana, the only apparent neutral, while the debate, lubricated with beer and *caipirinhas,* raged on the porch. Paulo led the opposition. It was understandable that, as the only man in the house, he should be protective. Toward evening the meal that Dona Joana had been all afternoon preparing was served, and the family had reached a verdict. Marco came and delivered it: Ana and I should correspond for a year, and if our love held that long, we could be married. Ana seemed to accept the decision, while I felt powerless and slightly bitter about the way the matter had been handled. I complimented Dona Joana on her fine cooking and apologized for not being hungry after all the trouble she had gone to. We left the party early, and with Tonho as chaperon drove in grim silence back to Sobradinho. "Look," he told me. "I think you're great. In fact I think you're super. But I've done a lot of traveling. I've driven trucks all over Brazil and sometimes was on the road three weeks at a time. And I know that the heart of a traveling man is never true. If it was up to me I'd say no. How do we know you're not going to get tired of her and ditch her after three months? After all, she's only twenty, and knows nothing about men."

Five months later, on the last day of Carnaval, I appeared at Iraci's door. A nearly fatal fever had struck me in Peru. After ten days of shuddering at a hundred and four degrees I had shaken it, but the bout had left me twenty pounds lighter and too weak and demoralized for further fieldwork. I returned to Brasília with my notebooks; Iraci had consented, just before I had left, to my marrying Ana when the trip was over. Shocked by my sallow and debilitated condition, Ana, Iraci, and Dona Joana outdid each other in the kitchen to put some weight back on me. Not only were three generations of Leonias women hovering over me, but Paulo's coolness toward me had thawed, and though he was not one to show his feelings, I could sense an undeclared familial supportiveness growing in him. A wedding date, April 9, was set. I rented a room from three sisters—Rufina, Alvina, and Regina—who lived several streets up from Iraci, and started writing The Rivers Amazon, as my book would be called. In the afternoon, to clear my head and get back my strength, I took long walks in the savanna. Ana kept commuting to FUNAI until a few weeks before the wedding, but I seldom went to the Plano except in the evening, to take her to a movie or dancing at the Salão de Samba. As I got to know Sobradinho, it became my adoptive primordial small town, a moving place for me because it was the sort of community I'd watch pass out of existence in my native Westchester County. I say small town, even though its population exceeded sixty thousand, because the people behaved in a way that was comparable to the inhabitants of an American town of several thousand. They were, furthermore, well integrated with trees and flowers and birds. In the "rurban" setting of Sobradinho, as a comparative study of the satellite cities described it, there was an almost ideal balance between man and nature, free of the misery of truly poor Brazil, yet without the manicured self-consciousness of our suburbs. The sigh of an earlier, happier time was audible.

The central rotary of the town was planted with yucca, or mother-in-law's tongue, as it is called popularly because of its serrated foliage. Some of the flower stalks were twenty feet high; some were broken over. The rotary was called Santos-Dumont Square. One did not challenge a Brazilian, especially in a bar, about whether Dumont was the Father of Aviation. In 1906 Dumont's eleventh flying machine became airborne; this was three years after the Wright Brothers' successful attempt, but Dumont didn't have to use a catapult. The mayor of Sobradinho's house had its own basketball court. It was built late in the previous decade to the specifications of the mayor at the time, who was Ana's basketball coach. The present mayor did not play basketball, and for the last few years the court had been sitting idle. The stores in Quadra 8, the shopping district, had colorful façades and Wild West lettering. The young men of Sobradinho hung out there, in tight-fitting pants that didn't allow pockets, so they carried their wallets in their hands. The wallets were equipped with a thong, as they are in the country at large, so they couldn't be yanked away by urchins, and they were usually heavy enough to serve as a blackjack should it be necessary to beat off an assailant. They were bulky not because they contained a lot of money, but because they were crammed

with the innumerable documents you had to be able to produce
at a moment's notice, particularly the identity card. Without
your *identidade* you were taken to jail, and because most people
in Sobradinho didn't have telephones, you stayed there until
your family realized that you were missing and came down to
the police station with your card to get you out. By then the
police had usually worked you over thoroughly. I remember
how alarmed Iraci was when Paulo didn't show up one night.
He turned out to have spent the night at Tété's.

The most popular juke joint in Quadra 8, La Cabana
Seresteira, had black walls with murals of dragons, cowboys,
and phoenixes. On the Saturday night we went there a live
band, for whom there was a fifty-cent *cover artístico*, played
samba and disco music. Teenage girls arrived in twos and
threes, hopeful yet afraid of being noticed; young soldiers with
shorn heads, on weekend passes, made up to lush older women.
By nightfall the room was full of smoke and bodies and glasses
being tapped to the whining of the electric guitar and the
wailing of the wa-wa pedal. Three police came in and asked for
identidades, and discovering a young man who was without his,
led him out of the joint and drove him away in a car. In front of
the joint, under a banner that said "Help the Flagelados," was a
flatbed truck with floral-painted sidepanels. There had been
flooding in the Northeast, and the local Lions Club was taking
donations of mattresses and clothing from the good people of
Sobradinho and throwing them on the truck.

Quadra 8 had all sorts of strange, tasty fruit and vegetables
with names like *chuchu, jamelão,* and *jabituvaca;* huge, leopard-
spotted catfish from the Amazon; coils of pungent black tobacco
called *fumo de corda;* fresh bread, and a wide assortment of dry
goods and notions. It was a place where a quarter still had
considerable purchasing power. One thing I couldn't find there
was dog food, although there were probably, by Paulo's

estimate, ten thousand dogs in Sobradinho. These animals had the same relationship with man that dogs had had for centuries; they attached themselves to a certain house and in return for scraps would shrilly announce the arrival of a stranger and appear ready to attack although they were in fact easily cowed by a raised voice or driven off with a stone. They were the "emaciated pariah dogs," in Paul Theroux's term, who roam through the third world. Infested with worms and yaws and predominantly hound, they were seldom petted or invited inside, and on the Planalto Central they replaced *urubús,* the vultures of northern Brazil, as the chief scavengers. In Sobradinho, their barks and yips, increasing in frenzy when the moon was full or a female in estrus, continued through the night. I saw an advertisement in a Brazilian magazine for canned dog food, but the product had yet to reach the District, as far as I could determine. Only "Dogui" kibbles were sold in bags at the supermarket in the Conjunto Nacional. Canned dog food represented a step in cultural evolution that Sobradinho hadn't yet taken.

Little disturbed the carefree, day-to-day life in Sobradinho, only the things that kept one awake at night: howling dogs, the penetrating whine of long-footed mosquitoes, the smell of the bone factory, where skeletons of cattle were broken down into phosphorus. It was a good place to see the famous Brazilian qualities, *alegria* and *calor humano,* cheerfulness and human warmth, at work. Not only the Leoniases, but every family I met there seemed close, and the love between members flowed uninhibitedly. One saw grown-up sisters holding hands as they walked down the red dirt lanes, and there were often three or four generations under one roof. The numerous churches in Sobradinho attested to the importance of religion in the citizens' lives. Some went to church to pray for miracles; it was the same motive that drove others to play the lotteries. Because Brazilians believe in miracles, they seem to happen with some regularity, and in the churches where hundreds have been cured of physical ailments, there is often a room where wax effigies of arms, legs, eyeballs, and other organs and limbs hang from the ceiling as testaments of miraculous healings. The hospitality one was likely to receive in the home of a Sobradinian was extraordinary. Visitors were always welcomed with a little cup of sweet black coffee and handed a plateful of whatever was cooking on the stove. The typical host dropped everything and sat and talked until the guests decided to leave, no matter how boring they were or how busy he was, and when they finally got up, he would invariably protest with a gentle look of anguish, *"Tá cedo. It's early."* The citizens of Sobradinho were mostly from the northern half of the country, where the population excels at hospitality, especially in the remote sections; in the Amazon the invitations I had received from backwoods people to stay with them were seriously meant to extend not for days but for months.

The work ethic of Sobradinho, Paulo explained one afternoon as we were walking up to Quadra 8, was also north Brazilian. "In the North," he said, "you work to eat; in the South you work to get ahead. Here in Sobradinho, everyone is *descansado* and *alegre* and feels sorry for the people in the Plano who have become *agitados, sistemáticos,* and often *neuróticos.* In the satellite cities work has only three objectives: to eat, to clothe yourself, and to have shoes on your feet." We passed an apricot-colored house from whose open window samba music was gushing. "And maybe," he was reminded, "to dance the samba." This ethic explained, in part, the lack of initiative of the Leonias males, why they had failed to capitalize on the opportunities of Brasília, why no one except Francisco was a professional. As long as they weren't actually going hungry, Paulo's uncles weren't about to bestir themselves. The Leonias women, on the other hand, were all hardworking and stably employed. This was typical of Latin American family dynamics. The male, to borrow an ornithological term, is altricial: he spends an inordinate amount of time in the nest, and for all his macho bravado, is unusually dependent upon women. Brazilian society is matrifocal; as in the other Catholic countries of Latin America, Mother Mary eclipses her son in the hierarchy of devotion, and as in Jamaica, the males "are permitted a degree of self-indulgence without domestic penalty, are physically pampered, get a thoroughness of attention unparalleled in Western culture," as the Jamaican journalist John Hearne writes. But as a result of their dependence they bear an unconscious resentment toward women that expresses itself in the frequency with which they make women pregnant and refuse to take responsibility for the issue, cheat on and otherwise abuse their wives, or leave them outright with a large family to support. Since the children of these unions grow up knowing only their mother or their grandmother, the pattern is self-perpetuating. In many of Sobradinho's families the father had been missing for some time. One man, however, was the head of two households, sometimes bedding down with a woman who lived on Iraci's street, and sometimes with her sister who lived several blocks up the hill. The children of this *ménage à trois,* who were both cousins and brothers and sisters, were clonelike carbon copies of each other, and got along famously.

I was particularly fond of two friends I made in Sobradinho during my closing days of bachelorhood. One was a sixty-year-old unpublished writer named Benito do Nascimento. Every morning he donned one of the two brown suits with wide lapels and white pinstripes issued him by the District government, walked up the hill, and caught the bus to the Plano, where he served coffee and ice water to the functionaries on the eleventh floor of the Buriti Palace annex. The *serventes* occupy the lowest station in Brasília's bureaucracy, but they are so well dressed that one could easily mistake them for their superiors, who are often in short sleeves and tieless. Benito had been living in the District for fifteen years, the last twelve of them in a *barraca* in Quadra 11 that he had built with wood begged from a nearby construction site. He had built a second *barraca* on the lot for his mother-in-law and allowed a friend to build a third one in back. Two of his rooms were rented out, and the rest of the house was inhabited by his family of thirteen. "I have this *numerosissima* family," he explained. "My youngest child is one and a half years old. I have to support them with seventeen hundred cruzeiros (less than a hundred and fifty dollars) a month. Is there any grace in that?" We were sitting in a small room that contained a dresser on which two tinted family portraits and a large new television set had been placed. In one of the drawers were Benito's manuscripts. He had been writing short stories for thirty years, but none of them had ever seen print. "No one has ever helped me," he complained. "When people get to the top they" (he ground his shoe on the floor as if stomping a cockroach) "do this to the rest." One of his early stories was called "No One Is a Patriot with an Empty Stomach" and was about his tour as a soldier in Rio Grande do Norte and the *flagelados* he saw there dying of hunger. The theme of another story, written a year after the 1964 revolution, "was that the authorities are appointed by God to punish the malefactors. I thought the authorities would like it, so I took it to the Ministry of Education to get the grammar corrected. But they put it in their archives and wouldn't give it back to me. Foolishly, I let them have the only copy I had." His latest story, "Feet Worth Millions," was about a famous soccer player who bore a strong resemblance to Pelé. I showed it to some Brazilians who were in a better position to judge the quality of the writing, and their consensus was that while the story was funny and in some places

111

moving, the style was too crude and full of misconstructions for it to be publishable. "Money is hard in this Brazil," Benito observed. "But I'll keep writing. I'm not going to keep my arms folded. As the proverb says,

> Agua molha na pedra dura
> Tanto bate até que fura.

"Soft water pounds on hard rock long enough until it cracks."

My other friend, Vincente, could usually be found of an evening playing the *cavaquinho* at his neighborhood bar. The *cavaquinho* has four steel strings and resembles a ukelele but is played like a mandolin. It is used as a rhythm instrument in samba music and as the lead instrument in another type of Brazilian music called *chorinho,* which was popular in the twenties and thirties and is now experiencing a revival. *Chorinho* means "little tearjerker" and refers to the weeping sound of the *cavaquinho,* which can be as affecting as the slow, moody solo of a Dixieland clarinet. It is a romantic music and like Dixieland is highly syncopated, with plenty of room for improvisation. A typical group consists of, besides the *cavaquinho,* a guitar or two, someone shifting sand or dried pinto beans back and forth in a steel canister called a *xeque-xeque,* someone else slapping a tambourine, and possibly a tenor saxophone. Jam sessions are called *potpourris* and are mainly given over to sentimental embellishments and mellow restatements of the melody line; but on a fast number the *cavaquinho* can break away with briskness of a bluegrass banjo. Vincente, who was about Benito's age, had been banging at his *cavaquinho* for forty years, as he put it. He knew dozens of slow, laid-back *chorinhos* and dozens of fast, staccato ones. I would show up at his bar some evenings, and taking my guitar, he would strum the chords of a *chorinho,* and I would write them down, then he would play lead while I, reading the progression, backed him up as best I could. Once he broke a string, and poking the blade of a penknife through the f-hole of his battered instrument, he pulled out an extra string which he had stored in the sound chamber. Then he removed the broken string and carefully wound the new one around its peg, and as he was bringing it up to pitch it snapped. In utter disgust he grabbed the remaining three strings, ripped the wooden bridge that held them in place from the face of the instrument, and stormed out of the bar. That had been his last extra string. The following evening he was back at the bar, meekly gluing his *cavaquinho* together.

With the wedding just a few weeks away, Iraci hired a girl to do the housecleaning so she could have more time for the preparations. Her name was Fatima and she had just come in from her aunt's farm in Goiás. A short, stubby, thick-thighed eighteen-year-old with a turned-up nose and two front teeth missing, she was illiterate and a *macumba* medium subject to sudden emotional seizures and uncontrollable fits of crying. Every morning for a dollar she would take all the furniture out of the house and put it in the garden and attack the floor with her mop, while country music blared from her transistor radio. Sometimes, when a favorite song was aired, she would stop scrubbing and samba with the mop. After she had finished cleaning the house she would sit in the doorway with the radio to her ear for an immobile hour or two. Once she showed me two rattles from a rattlesnake she had killed on her aunt's farm. She kept them wrapped in a handkerchief. Ground into powder they were a remedy, she said, for toothache. At night she would make herself up, put on her good dress, and walk up the hill to the elementary school, where she had enrolled in a reading class. But she made no progress either at learning to read or at finding a boyfriend, which we all suspected was her real interest in attending, and after a month she gave up on city life and returned to her aunt's farm.

The only church which, for a tidy sum, would marry a

divorced foreigner to a Brazilian, was the Catholic Church of Brazil. The marriage would not be legal in Brazil, but at least there would be a ceremony that Ana's family could attend. A second ceremony would have to be performed in the United States, and Ana would enter the country as my "alien fiancée." The bishop, whose name was Dom Luís, explained that in order to be married I would have to join the Church, and so, along with two other couples, we attended six classes with him. Dom Luís was a portly, rubicund man who wore a purple cap and grey vestments over a white shirt whose cuffs were frayed. His lectures were a mixture of incomprehensible theology and pragmatic directives. At his final lecture he asked the women to leave the room. "A woman gets used to your smell," he told the three imminent grooms. "She knows when you come home if another woman has even slightly touched you. She can tell by instinct when you touch her if your soul is in it. Women have something in this department that we don't. Even if you take a shower she can tell it was with a different soap than the one in the house." Then, with graphic gestures, he lectured us on how to make a woman happy. "Another thing," he said in closing, "is variety. You don't want to get into *monotonia*. Otherwise you fall into *routina.*" Then he sent us out and brought in the women. "Always look your best," he told them. "Dress well. Get your hair done once a week. Be *bem preparada* to meet you husband."

We were married the day before Easter, on Alleluia Saturday. I had never seen Ana so radiant as when she came down the aisle on Paulo's arm, with a gleeful throng of little cousins running behind. My witnesses were Armando and the truck driver and Betty the FUNAI librarian. Armando had stood as my godfather at my baptism the Sunday before. Marco and Tété, who were Ana's witnesses, also gave the reception, as there was more room at their house than at Iraci's. Most of the sixty guests were blood relatives and to seat them all we had brought over, in Armando's truck, a couple of dozen dimunitive desks and chairs from the school where Iraci taught. We had gotten a keg of beer and hired a woman whose *kibis,* meat patties reminiscent of piroshkis, were famous in Sobradinho, to cater the party. In addition, there were shishkabobs and ears of corn and a memorable wedding cake with a lot of fresh fruit inside and large enough for everyone to have a sliver. A one-eyed accordionist named Graca, who came from Floriano, furnished the music. She had brought along a torrid trumpeter and a vocalist who got more sounds out of a tambourine than I had thought was possible. Graca's fingers flew over the keys and with everyone dancing the *forró* the shindig went till dawn, long after we had left for our honeymoon in Bahia. Dona Joana's distinguished-looking brother João Nepomuceno, who had given up his floating restaurant and was living in São Paulo, insisted that we leave the reception as soon as the cake had been cut and the photographer had finished documenting the occasion. Our wedding pictures, now preserved in a leather-bound album, evoke a world that, in its solidity and simplicity, Americans I have shown it to can scarcely believe existed in 1976; they all think the photographs were taken in the 1940s. "Go now, my children," Uncle Joe said as he shooed us into the Variant, and Dona Joana started to cry; like an Indian she always cried at the leavings and returnings of those who are dear to her. "You have taken one of the flowers out of my garden," she told me.

Part Three

B rasília's great scenic asset is its sky. In the absence of
mountains, the clouds are towering snowpeaks; in the
absence of the sea, the sky is oceanic in its ever-changing
vastness. Each day, from the moment the sun surfaces in the
low-lying mists to the moment it slips delicately behind the
horizon, a new drama is presented in the sky. The actors are
always the same—epic clouds, portentous shafts of light, ashen
curtains of rain, red veins of lightning, rolling choruses of
thunder—but no performance is ever repeated. The action
begins when the sun gets high enough to burn off the mist.
There are few clouds as yet, only scattered fragments of *Cumulus
humilis*. A sky with only *Cumulus humilis* means fair weather; at
sea, a group of them in the distance means an island. In
Brasília, during the "winter" from June to August, when there
is little rain, the sky is cloudless all day, or it may contain, by
late afternoon, a few shreds hardly even deserving the rank of
Cumulus humilis which disappear, in any case, by the following
morning. But during most of the year, as the sun moves higher
into the sky, the air becomes increasingly heavy with moisture.
Columns of vapor ascend wherever two opposing winds converge and wherever the soil is most responsive to the sun's
differential heating. Throughout the morning and into the

119

afternoon unseen but massive evaporation continues. By late afternoon the little puffs have swollen into colossal nebulosities, laterally into *Cumulus congestus* and vertically into cumulonimbus. A few thunderheads in the District have been estimated to be eighteen kilometers from foot to anvil-headed summit, and once, as I was driving in from Sobradinho, I saw a single *Cumulus congestus,* perhaps ten miles from tip to tip, hovering over the capital and threatening to burst. The afternoon rains are short-lived and torrential, in typical tropical fashion, and they are convective in origin, unlike the orographic and frontal rains of the temperate regions. So intense are they that in twenty minutes up to 1.2 inches may fall. The cul-de-sacs in the *superquadras* are converted into sluices of muddy red water whose force has elsewhere opened, here and there on the plateau, deep, jagged lines that seem like earthquake gullies but are in fact *voçorocas,* erosion gullies. The extraordinary thing about the rain is that it never seems to penetrate. There is no lingering wetness when it stops, and never, even at the height of rainy season, is the air oppressively humid, but always fresh and clean, a delight to draw into the lungs. Many of the rains are purely local. Sudden showers move from hill to hill, and while the North Wing of the Plano may be experiencing a thunderous downpour, the South will be bathed in sunlight. One moment you need sunglasses, the next to turn on the wipers of your car, as you pass people who have taken hasty refuge from the slanting rain by leaning against the lee sides of eucalyptus trees. I have spent hours watching and photographing the mood changes of the plateau. In its twenty-mile vistas several unrelated meteorological displays often take place at once. In one part of the sky, a black screen of rain sifts down from a *Cumulus congestus;* elsewhere, a hilltop is fixed in a beam of light that streams down from a break in a cumulonimbus. As the clouds swell and part and regroup again, windows through which rays of unblocked sunlight slant down are always opening. On overcast days the sun is seldom seen and only its glare, filtering through the cloud layers, is felt. On clear days the lower layers are empty and feathery wisps of cirrostratus, interlocking filaments of *Cirrus fibratus,* and thin, luminous veils of pure cirrus, composed of ice crystals, are visible in the upper troposphere, perhaps twenty thousand feet up. Once I experienced a *chuva do sol,* an odd, Magritte-like phenomenon in which rain fell in full sunlight. No clouds were directly overhead, but one whose precipitation was swept away by a strong wind before it could reach the ground must have been in the vicinity.

The best cloudscapes are in September and October and again in April and May, transitional periods between the wet and dry seasons. During the *verão,* the "summer" between November and March, the cloud cover is usually too solid for spectacular individuals. The plateau gets more rain then than even the rain forest, except during the sporadic *veranicos,* or "little summers," when an intense spurt of solar activity creates a shortage of rain for one to fifteen days, during which temperatures rise and crops can be decimated. During the *verão* the continent is hotter than the surrounding seas, and there is a monsoon effect, as humid air is drawn into the interior from over the waters. In the *inverno,* the opposite happens: In June the anticyclone that stays east of the continent, over the Atlantic, for most of the year, starts to move west until its center is more or less over Brasília, and this high-pressure system becomes a source of outflowing cool, dry air. During this period the monthly rainfall averages less than half an inch in July when, for as long as records have been maintained, it has never rained once. With little moisture in the soil, the plateau absorbs the full, sensible heat of the sun until by midwinter it has become a parched semidesert. Huge dust columns, whirling erect eddies called *redemoinhos,* microtornadoes three hundred, even a thousand feet high, "like pilasters holding up the infinite sky of the Planalto," as Juscelino described them, traverse the savanna.

121

Due to the dust there is a marked increase in cases of bronchial disorder at this time of the year, and the sound of coughing is heard frequently. Juscelino wrote eloquently of the "omnipresent" and "dictatorial" dust. "Over that world of scaffolding, of metal riggings of forests of cranes, an element pontificated which, like a noxious weed, frayed nerves, intoxicated lungs, inflamed eyes. It was the dust—a dust such as only exists in Brasília—red and fine, with an extraordinary capacity to impregnate, and always present in everything one touched. It was in the water one drank, in the air one breathed, on the pillow where one laid one's head."

Toward evening in the *inverno* dendritic bolts of heat lightning branch down, but with little effect. Because the resins of the trees, unlike those of our northwestern pines, are incombustible, the savanna has never been ignited by a lightning strike, though plenty of trees have been scorched or cloven. By night the relative humidity rises and as in the desert, the temperature plunges as much as twenty centigrade degrees; both the hottest and the coldest readings are recorded in the *inverno*. Most of the year, however, the climate hovers at a balmy sixty-nine degrees Fahrenheit, with 60 percent humidity.

Many sober travelers, among them Darwin, Lévi-Strauss, and Aldous Huxley, have spoken highly of the South American sunsets. I don't know why they should be more remarkable there than the sunsets on other continents, but they do seem to be; and nowhere are they more sensational than on the Planalto Central. By the time the sun is ready to go down on the plateau the various types of cumulus have grown to maximum impressiveness, like flowers at the height of bloom, and as the ones in the west roll and redouble, horizontal shafts of rose light break through the gaps as if shot from a projection booth, and traveling all the way across the sky, fire up, in bands of varying intensity, the high, translucent veils of cirrus. After this initial, pink phase, the sunset proceeds to a more violent, orange one, at

122

whose climax opalescent plumes of vapor escape from the crests of the clouds in brilliant arcs and tangents, and the whole western sky is too unbearably aflame to look upon. Then, in the last, purple phase, the disc sinks quickly, but its reflected light lingers for another twenty minutes or so, steadily weakening, receding westward from the edges of the clouds. Often, on the way somewhere, I would stop to photograph an arresting cloud or an exquisite sunset. It was all right that I arrived late, for the people I was going to meet were usually late, too.

Someone with a solitary, contemplative bent cannot help responding to the steppelike vastness of the Planalto. Wordsworth undoubtedly would have liked it. Judging from the returns of questionnaires that have been circulated among them, the citizens of Brasília respond to it, but from their car or apartment windows; few venture out into it. Brazilians' appreciation of nature, as a whole, is still largely on an unconscious level. That it exists is evinced by the popularity of houseplants and caged birds, among other things, but the conscious preoccupation, the job at hand, is to acquire Western technology, and they are still so ubiquitously confronted with those enemies of progress, the wild and the primitive, that they do not yet hold them in particular esteem. Nature in the raw is still something to be feared, conquered, and eradicated. The ecological movement is just starting to appear. A few dedicated conservationists in the government are laboring over a national parks system that is still largely on paper, and there is growing concern about the Amazon in the educated sector of the population, like the pediatrician in Brasília who spoke of "the barbarous and senseless destruction of our resources" that he had heard was going on there. But few have been to the Amazon or know anything about the region; those who can travel go abroad. Exaggerated reports by foreign scientists of the extent of the deforestation, furthermore, have reduced the credibility of the movement in Brazil. It is to be hoped that Brazilians realize in time the point of these warnings. "Only elitists, people with high ideas, become ecology-minded," an important minister told me. "The entire uproar is just a by-product of sophistication and technological advance."

Another cultural barrier to proximity with nature is the previously mentioned gregariousness; in both indigenous and modern Brazil, no one is alone by choice, and the pursuit of solitude is regarded as peculiar behavior. Jogging and bicycling haven't caught on yet in the District, though the plateau is an ideal place for them. Whenever I announced that I was going for a walk in the savanna, therefore, I was generally asked, "What on earth for?" and "Don't you want someone to go with you?" I was warned that the savanna was filled with snakes, but in the hours I spent wandering in it, I never met one. It is true that there are deadly species on the Planalto, including fer-de-lances, rattlers, and corals, but the snakes there are as reticent as they are in most places. My favorite walk was a little-used five-mile dirt road which ascends the northern rim of the Sobradinho valley and leads to a place called Fercão, where there is a large plant that produced most of the concrete and asphalt used in the construction of the capital. Early in 1979, when Ana and I returned to Brasília for a two-month visit, I caught a ride to Fercão one morning with my godfather, Armando Marchioretto, in his yellow dumptruck. Armando's parents had migrated from Padua. With his five brothers he owned a thousand-*alqueire* ranch in Mato Grosso (an *alqueire* is roughly one-third of an acre). But in 1971 he was unable to stand his wife's unfounded fits of jealousy any longer, and leaving in the night he made his way to Brasília with only two hundred cruzeiros in his pocket. Armando had no formal education but he was a hard worker and a quick learner, and Brasília was a good place to begin a new life. He started out driving a tractor for room and board, which wasn't much, but with the experience and a letter of recommendation he was hired as a truck driver by a construction firm. By 1973 he had saved enough to buy an old dumptruck and go independent. Several trucks later he was half-owner of a 1974 Alfa Romeo and full owner of a new car and a house in Sobradinho; he was doing well, a mild-mannered forty-one-year-old with glasses, a thin mustache, and a large Adam's apple to make up for a lack of chin. He and Iraci had known each other for six years. In 1972 she was teaching in a school at Fercão, and Armando would often give the teachers a ride back to Sobradinho. She was the last of the teachers to get off.

The availability of sand and gravel from Fercão was an important factor in the selection of Brown as a practicable site for the capital. Much of the hill behind the plant had been blasted away to become the stuff of *superquadras* and asphalt roads, but Armando estimated there was still enough of it left to supply Brasília with material for a hundred years. Depending on the demand he made one to four runs a day to construction sites, with five hundred cubic feet of number two or three crushed grey rock, red clay lateritic pebbles, or pulverized calcareous dust. At the moment a lot of building was going on. On the road to the Plano we had passed truck after truck with helmeted laborers in back, sitting in plywood shacks, along with women who would do the cooking. I drank a cup of coffee with Armando and the other drivers who were waiting for the plant to start up, then struck off along the Córrego de Fercão, a small creek lined with buriti palms and rural huts of various construction. At a mud-and-wattle *casebra* with a buriti-palm-thatch roof, I stopped and spoke with a woman who was sweeping her yard with a homemade buriti palm-wisp broom. Her name was Maria Magdalena. "I came here five years ago from Goiás. Two years ago my husband left me for another shameless dog," she said, her lower lip aquiver, her face already hardened at thirty-three. Every day she left her four children, the youngest of whom could be heard crying inside the hut, to wash clothes in

Sobradinho. She had three clients. Her oldest boy fished the creek for small catfish. The papaya tree in the yard was hers, but the chickens running loose belonged to the other people who lived in the hut. She pointed to their room. Dozens of sandflies were biting us, and I was eager to keep walking. In forty-five minutes I had gained the ridge, with a fine view of the Sobradinho valley.

The rock of central Brazil is part of a crystalline massif called the Brazilian Shield, and is among the most ancient on earth, dating to the Archean period. It is mostly igneous, or volcanic, in origin, and about two-thirds covered with sedimentary bands of limestone, sandstone, and shale, many of which are folded and deformed. The plateau was formed by wind erosion, which sheared the rock until it was absolutely level. Later, rain ate through the weaker sedimentary layers and washed them away, leaving domelike hills or *chapadas* of obdurate crystalline rock. Across the valley, some fifteen miles away, I could see a prominence called the Chapada de Contagem, which partitions Sobradinho from the Plano. Years ago, when the District consisted of several vast semifeudal ranches called *latifúndios,* at the end of a drive the cowboys would assemble all the cattle on the Chapada de Contagem, where they were branded and divided, the cowboys getting one calf for every three that the owner kept for himself. The plateau is technically described as a dissected pediplain. Most of it is suavely undulating but here, at the head of the valley, the effects of erosion were dramatic. The terrain was ruffled with deep ravines and sheer green hills whose slopes were ribbed like fans. Such sudden breaks in the landscape are known as *quebradas.* The hillsides were gleaming with freshets and coated with velvet grass. The ravines were choked with gallery forest, miniature jungles that are floristically related to both the coastal and the Amazon rain forests. Gallery forest is a sign of water. It lines streams and sprouts

126

about springs. Several kinds of monkeys—capuchins, howlers, marmosets—swing from the branches.

I examined the cross-section of a hill which the road had cut through. In some violent upheaval the thin laminations of yellow-green slate, with a subtle tracery of blue and orange lines meandering through them, had been tilted ninety degrees from their original angle of deposition until they stood vertical. Not far beneath the slate, there would have to be granite, perhaps metamorphosed into schist or serpentine. The foot of red laterite above the slate was typical of the soil of central Brazil. It ranges in grain size from knuckle-sized boulders to colloid clay whose invisible particles become the dust of the dry season. Such fine weathering is itself an indication of the plateau's antiquity.

I wondered if at some point in the complex geological history of this *quebrada* any crystals had been formed. They are found elsewhere on the plateau, in volcanic dikes called pegmatites where the cooling down of molten magma was slow enough for individual minerals to separate and grow in bristling clusters along the edges of the seam. The nearest pegmatite of consequence is about sixy miles southwest of Brasília. A small, opportunistic settlement called Cristalina has arisen on it. Thirty miles from any neighbor, Cristalina has one industry and one raison d'être: the extraction and lapidation of gem crystals. It has thirty-six stores with glittering trays of amethyst, aquamarine, garnet, citrine, topaz, morganite, tourmaline, kunzite, rubelite, chrysolite, and other polished, faceted semiprecious stones. The prospector who mines the crystals gets practically nothing for his effort, but by the time they have reached the boutiques at the Hotel Nacional in Brasília, the bits of colored rock have risen many times in value. More than a hundred boys stand on the road before Cristalina, holding up crystals they have dug up themselves. On March 19, 1979, two boys on the road were shot dead by a man who fled on foot into the savanna and later confessed to being in the hire of the town's gem merchants, who were upset at the way the boys had been cutting into their business. In Brazil, each profession has its associated stone. My mother-in-law, for example, wears a green tourmaline ring. Secretaries are entitled to rose tourmaline. Dieticians sport amethyst, members of the telecommunications industry have blue sapphire, bacteriologists emeralds, economists aquamarines. As a journalist I would be eligible for a ruby.

The savanna of central Brazil is known as the *cerrado;* between 694,000 and 772,000 square miles of the country are *cerrado;* it is the second great life realm in Brazil after the Amazon forest, with 965,000 square miles. Many people have remarked how much the *cerrado* resembles the savannas of Africa, and indeed there are intriguing correlations between its fauna and certain genera of African savanna trees, which are part of the abundant evidence that the two continents were once connected. For an environment that is rated "extreme" because of both the extreme poverty of its soil and the severity of its dry season, the *cerrado* has a surprisingly rich flora, upwards of eight thousand higher plant species. George Eiten, an American botanist at the University of Brasília, has counted 180 species of vascular plants on a single two-thousand-square-foot patch of *cerrado,* but that was an exceptional find, he admitted; the normal density, about two or three hundred species per hectare (a hectare is 2.47 acres) is still impressive when compared with other plant communities. The *cerrado* is rich in species (there are, for example, 148 kinds of terrestrial orchid alone) because the Central Plateau has been continuously available for plant occupation throughout the whole Tertiary Period, some ninety million years—for as long as there have been flowering plants, in other words. While other surfaces were periodically flooded or covered by ice, the vegetation of the *cerrado* was permitted to speciate in peace. But the harshness of the environment inhibited its growth forms. Only small, warped trees do well in the *cerrado*. Their thick, corky bark protects them from sun, fire, and insects. Their stiff, broad leaves are covered with a waxy cuticle that prevents water from escaping. Their extensive root systems reach down to deep, always moist layers of soil. Their stunted size may be due to the abundance of aluminum in the soil, which has a toxic effect on plants. But what makes them contorted is not yet understood. The mechanism is clear: after a burst of healthy growth the tips of the stems suddenly die, the terminal branches take over as the leader, and as the bark grows thicker it covers over the evidence that the grotesquely twisted branches are actually a series of stems. But what makes the stem die, and what the advantage of tortuosity could possibly be, no one has even hypothesized. Few other woodlands, perhaps only the elfin cloud forests in the Andes and the katanga woodland in Zaire, have trees as small and contorted as the ones in the *cerrado*.

I noticed the irridescent blue wings of a morpho butterfly flashing in a gully. Then the bird-sized insect leaped up in front of me, and bobbing erratically, continued down the road. I would have liked to take its picture but the morphos are such strong fliers that even birds don't try to run them down. Were it not for a fatal weakness—they are irresistibly drawn to specimens of themselves which morpho hunters set out as decoys—they would not be so badly persecuted. Morpho wings, placed under the glass of ashtrays, cocktail trays, and landscapes made entirely of butterfly parts, are a staple item in the Latin American tourist trade. I spent the next few hours stalking more cooperative species with my zoom lens. There are about twelve hundred species in the *cerrado*, half the number in the Amazon. The most visible butterflies here, as in most of the New World tropics, are the heliconians. One often sees the blurred flurry of their brown and orange wings in people's gardens. Once I saw a heliconian, or one of its many mimics, fluttering around in the

Conjunto Nacional, in a store that carried bolts of cloth and leather handbags. It must have sailed in from the plain, attracted by the neon lighting. Heliconian larvae feed on passionflower vines, whose alkaloids make them toxic. Birds have learned to shun lazily flapping, elongate, two-tone wings, and the heliconians are simulated by dozens of other unrelated species which are either perfectly palatable or toxic themselves; they can be told apart only by examination of their body size, genitalia, wing venation, and subtle differences in coloration. New subspecies are constantly adopting the heliconian look and the heliconians themselves are among the most plastic creatures; one species alone has some twenty-five different forms. Because they produce three to five broods a year their mutations can actually be observed, offering a rare opportunity for the student of evolution. Since the Pleistocene Epoch, when the firsst known heliconians appeared, there have been sixty thousand or so generations of them, so they have had time to change and change and change again.

After a long chase I finally got a butterfly to hold still. It was small, with brilliant red and blue uppersides, and the numeral "88" inscribed by dots and wavering black lines on its white hindwing undersides. It was resting on a tree in the tomato family called fruit-of-the-wolf, a common weed tree whose fruit is in fact eaten by wolves, where there are still wolves. A few maned wolves still roam in the savannas of the Federal District. I have never seen one—few have—but have found their rusty hairs entangled in barbed wire and their scat, filled with fruit-of-the-wolf seeds. None of the large native mammals are easy to see except perhaps the pampas deer. Without an all-out effort one must be satisfied with proof of their existence: a termitary recently demolished by an armadillo; the footprint of a giant anteater, which looks like those of a child; the three-toed hoofprint of a tapir, with a spread of up to five inches; the well-traveled path of capybara, the mastiff-sized rodent, in the tall grass along a gallery forest. All these animals have been forced into hiding by dog packs, composed of larger feral canines who have found the savanna more to their liking than the satellite cities. In many cases the slaughtered victim is left untouched; the dogs seem to hunt for the fun of killing. About the only place where the wildlife survives in quantity is the National Park of Brasília, a pristine, hundred-and-twenty-thousand-acre tract that comes up to the northern edge of the city. The park is fenced and two guards patrol its borders in a Volkswagen Xavante (the Xavante are a fierce Amazonian tribe, like our Comanche, and the Volkswagen Xavante is a kind of four-wheel-drive dune buggy), shooting any dogs that try to get in.

The next butterfly I photographed didn't have to have its confidence won over; it chased me, and I was able to get a shot of it on my pantleg. It was one of the "clickers," emitting a rapid series of loud, sharp clicks in flight. "The butterfly makes this sound by snapping two body segments together while moving both pairs of wings in a peculiar alternating beat," Thomas C. Emmel explained. The young Charles Darwin, traveling in central Brazil, was intrigued by the snaps, and conjectured that they might be a "startle" mechanism to confuse attackers. Actually, they are more likely to be related to courtship and territorial defense. The rest of the insect's behavior certainly seemed territorial: it went after everything that violated its air space: me, a stray dog, a black and red swallowtail which it pursued from a distance of several inches, clicking vigorously. Its flight pattern, which I sat and observed for a while, seemed more in the nature of a temporary territorial circuit than the apparently random darting about of other butterflies. After a considerable pause ten feet up and facedown on a vochysia tree it would fly over to a slate outcrop, rest there awhile, then fly into a corky little tree with particularly thick twigs and leaves the consistency of cardboard; and finally return to its original station on the vochysia, with whose bark the intricate grey, black, and white patches on its open wings blended nicely. The vochysia was almost thirty feet tall. Its branching was less impulsive and more graceful than that of the other trees, and it had saved all its leaves for its crown. Vochysias are the tallest trees in the *cerrado,* and their crowns are the favorite perches of toucans, magpies, guira cuckoos, caracaras, and other birds who require a view. There was, in fact, a caracara perched in the highest point of this vochysia. The *cerrado* does not lack for birds of prey, but of the many kinds of hawks, vultures, and kites that frequent it, the golden-headed, fiercely regal caracara is the most often seen, and the most deserving candidate for lord of the savanna. It is both a hunter and a scavenger, whose diet ranges from grasshoppers to dead wild dogs. Shielding my face for a moment against the blinding heat, I looked up again and the caracara was gone. Stillness, except for trembling grass and my own heart pounding. The glare was overpowering and with the sun near its zenith the temperature must have been well in the nineties. I thought of how Meursault in Camus' novel shot the Arab on the beach, not really because he was menacing him, but because in the swimming Algerian heat nothing seemed to matter. My first encounter with that book, in a prep-school French course, had shaken me. When I learned that nothing mattered, I stopped wearing ties and started skipping morning chapel and was only allowed to return to school for my senior year after I had written a letter to the Rector assuring him that I had straightened out. Existentialism, it seems, fares better in the tropics. I sat down under the vochysia, took out my notebook, and began to write. "In a hot tropical sun it is easy to believe in a kind of biological existentialism: that I am an agglomeration of matter, assimilated or reconstituted from other organisms and somehow, miraculously, possessed of a consciousness informed by genes, culture, education, family-induced patterns of behavior; that this consciousness is hopelessly flawed and limited; that I am in constant competition with other organisms, and

132

that there can be only temporary alliances for the purpose of consolidation or advancement. Beyond this it is hard to believe. The evidence on every level, from plants to politics, is too overwhelming. Within this dark frame, of course, there are frequently surprising flashes of light and color—the unsolicited human kindness, the freshness of new morning, the love of a woman. One should always be prepared to have one's view of life swept away by fresh evidence." At my feet I noticed, resting on a blade of sedge, a minuscule Ericinid butterfly, brown with white spots, and hovering over it with my zoom lens, I photographed it drinking intently from a dewdrop with its proboscis fully unfurled. Normally the proboscis is coiled like a party blower.

Where the road began its descent into the valley, I left it and struck out across the savanna. I wanted to follow the scarp for a few more miles and to come down through the meadow behind Iraci's house. From hidden positions in my immediate vicinity I kept hearing shrill, faint tintinabulations. They sounded exactly as if a hostess at a dinner party were shaking a small crystal bell. Wading stealthily through the grass I was surprised to find that the bell cricket, or *gafanhoto*, which produces these sounds, is a small, nondescript orthopteran, in comparison with the four-inch-long emerald grasshopper which springs up from the *cerrado* and flies awkwardly for short distances. The tinkling is a by-product of its whirring wings. A few hundred yards off several *seriemas* were engaged in a squawking bout. They were about the size of egrets, with long red legs, long necks, and heads like hawks except for the crests that had sprouted whimsically at the base of their bills. Their raucous noises, rising and falling in volume and pitch, reminded me of mad, hysterical laughter. The *seriema* eats rats, reptiles, and insects and occupies the approximate niche of the American roadrunner, though it belongs to a different family. It is particularly fond of surprising snakes basking in the road and relies more on its legs than its capacity for flight, though, when pressed, it will take to the air with slow, heronlike wingbeats. Once Waldemar and I chased a *seriema* down a back road in the Variant and clocked it, in full stride, at forty miles per hour. When he hunted the birds in Piauí he noticed that their squawking was especially exuberant after a rain, and thought that it must be an expression of pleasure, as the sun dried their wings.

As I drew near the place where the *seriemas* had been calling, they of course stopped, and I was left in the silence of strange vegetation, unlike anything I had seen in the temperate zone, or anywhere. Hundreds of bizarre plants in the pipewort family had flowered several feet above the grass. Their hoary influores-cence was the shape of a dandelion head gone to seed, but many times magnified, which had sprouted on the tips of four-inch shafts a halo of little white and black buttons, the white buttons being new flowers and the black ones those that were already beginning to pass. In the center of one of the influorescences there was a metallic green sheen—a buprestid beetle. The pipeworts gave way to a sparse forest of even more bizarre treelets whose local name, according to a boy I met in the savanna who also told me he walked three hours to school every day, is rhea-shinbone, named after the largest bird of the region. Each rhea-shinbone has several woody, grey stalks which may or may not branch before producing, at their tips, a sheaf of swordlike leaves. The new leaves come out in groups of two and are incorporated into the salads of the people who live in the savanna. In May the treelets produce a striking lilac flower with a yellow center which is soon devoured by ants. The rhea-shinbone is partial to shallow, rocky soil. It belongs to a family of some hundred and fifty species that are partial to the semidry parts of South America and Africa. One hill in Minas Gerais has half the known species in the family growing on it. I have never inspected the rhea's tibia at close range but I expect it is stout and grey like the stalks of the treelets. The rhea, which resembles the African ostrich, is much hunted in the *cerrado* and getting very scarce. Standing as high as five feet, they are the largest bird in the New World, though the Andean condor has the greatest wingspan. I saw one in 1976, in Brasília Park, for several seconds before it bounded into a stand of rhea-shin-bones, and none in 1979. At the beginning of the rains, when there is an abundance of insects and grain to fuel the rigors of courtship and reproduction, the cock rounds up five or six females, scrapes out of the ground a nest about a yard in diameter, and lines it with grass. The females lay twenty to fifty yellow-green eggs in it on which the cock sits, and after they hatch, he jealously guards the warren, even against his harem, until the chicks are ready to go off on their own some six weeks later.

On the other side of the thicket I came to a hilltop that had been cleared, the savanna trees pulled up by the roots to prevent their sprouting again, and neat rows of pine seedlings left in their place. The agricultural and silvicultural potential of the *cerrado* has suddenly, in the last year or two, become the subject of excited discussion. With the hopes of opening the Amazon to large-scale agriculture largely dashed by the dismal results of farming schemes along the Transamazon Highway, many are now turning to the *cerrado,* which is about 60 percent arable, as the new frontier. The main beneficiaries of "reforestation" (a term I find as offensive as "reclaiming," since both imply utter insensitivity to the value of native ecosystems) are Caribbean pine and eucalyptus. Some farmers are wildly enthusiastic about eucalyptus; a quick cash crop, it is steadily supplanting the forests of southern Brazil and gives the best return to the tree-farmer. Its detractors complain of the loss of native plants of unknown genetic and pharmacological promise, a significant portion of which have yet to be even identified. Eucalyptus saplings, they also point out, require a great deal of water, and by lowering the water table and desiccating the ground, they increase the hazard of fire. I find it hard to despise the trees, not to be refreshed by the menthol of their crushed leaves, or charmed by their woody seed capsules, which seem like buttons from a tweed coat, each incised with a cross. No other tree has been so successful a colonist, thriving in so many parts of the world. For this I think the eucalyptus deserves begrudging respect. A few of the trees, judiciously planted here and there, with the silver undersides of their foliage tossed up as in a Gainsborough painting, are a pleasant relief to the flat monotony of the *cerrado*.

But the main thrust for the exploitation of the Central Plateau is agronomic. Many Brazilian scientists, looking ahead to the crushing food shortages predicted for the twenty-first century, see Brazil, with its constant growing season and its vast untouched terrain, emerging as a world producer, and the focus of production may be the *cerrado*. A more immediate objective is to make the Federal District self-sufficient with respect to its own food supply. Sixty percent is still trucked in from São Paulo. I spent a morning with Ilario Kappes, a young agronomist who had left Rio Grande do Sul to join a farm cooperative in Brasília. As we drove through rustling seas of soybean, in which a few token trees had been left as "souvenirs," Kappes raved about the *cerrado*. "Here everything that grows in the South does well, except apples: peaches, grapes, figs, olives, garlic, onions, tomatoes, melons, peppers, soybean, rice; and everything that grows in the North does well, too: banana, manioc, cane, mango, cashew, coffee, passionfruit. All you need is irrigation and fertilizer. There's plenty of water, even in the dry season, if you go down far enough, and after enrichment with potassium, phosphorus, zinc, calcium, and magnesium, the soil compares with the best of them. Why, our soybean yields are half again what they're getting in Rio Grande do Sul. And ten years ago, everybody said this was a desert." The best-yielding crops so far have been soybean and dry rice, which are grown in the wet season; between June and August, wheat is planted. The forty associates of the cooperative all had German or Japanese names, I gathered from signs identifying the crops: MODULE 10, KAZUYUSHI KOYAMA; MODULE 4, SMIDIO KLEIN. "The Brazilian native," Kappes explained, "is lazy. He can't be motivated to anything but subsistence agriculture—a little garden, a few head of cattle. It's a cultural problem. You have heard the expression: in the midst of blind people a man with one eye is a king."

In the middle of the pine plantation I came to a large, temporary shelter, such as the Indians construct. Under the shade of palm-thatch twenty men were taking their midday meal. They were migrant laborers from the Northeast. Their boss was called an *empreiteiro,* or subcontractor. The hill had been cleared in exactly the manner in which the Amazon forest is being taken down: the large rancher subcontracts the work to *empreiteiros,* who come in with gangs of *nordestinos. "Vamos almoçar,"* said the *empreiteiro,* handing me a plate of gruel. "Let's eat!" After passing around the contents of my sidebag, guavas from the yard of Iraci's neighbor, and taking a long drink from the spring that rose beside the hut, I continued up and over the parched hilltop. Even the termitaries had been razed. But they would be back. I have seen a mature stand of eucalyptus "reclaimed" by their three-foot red belljars. As earthworms are in the deciduous woods and ants in the rain forest, termites are the chief earth-movers and decomposers of organic material in the *cerrado.* The *cerrado* is singularly blessed with termites. Up to eight hundred mounds per hectare, with several million termites in each belonging to as many as eleven genera, have been counted. The genera are named for outstanding physical or behavioral traits. *Velocitermes* is highly active, *Bellicositermes* highly aggressive. *Cyranotermes,* named for Cyrano de Bergerac, has a long nasus, or tube extending from the center of its head that fires out defensive secretions. The heads of the soldier caste of *Constrictotermes* are pinched just behind the antenna. *Diversitermes* has three separate soldier forms. *Ruptitermes* has no soldiers at all, and the colony is defended by workers who, contracting their abdominal muscles, intentionally burst their intestines so that attacking ants can be immobilized by the shiny fluid which is thus spread about. To these workers, the survival of the colony is more important than that of oneself—one of numerous indications that termite society is more advanced than ours in terms of altruism and cohesiveness, if not individual intelligence. The mound itself is a kind of superorganism, and should an armadillo or an anteater break one open with its powerful claws, the colony, with its elaborate social order and strict division of labor, simply falls apart. The individuals scatter, and wandering aimlessly across the savanna are soon fallen upon by their predators. The outer walls of *cupinzeiros,* as the termite hills are called, are cemented together from bits of regurgitated soil, grass, and wood. They are rock-hard and several inches thick, but finely porous to allow the escape of carbon dioxide and the entry of oxygen. Numerous other organisms inhabit *cupinzeiros:* ants and aphids (both of whose larvae get a free meal by mimicking larval termites), scorpions, spiders, snakes, lizards, and small marsupials; the campo flicker drills a nesting hole in its walls. Some eat termites; some eat things that eat termites; some simply find the *cupinzeiro* cooler, safer, and damper than the *cerrado.* Standing in the savanna, one is hardly ever more than twenty yards from a *cupinzeiro.* The more evolved species live on the ground, foraging dead leaves, seeds, and blades of grass. They forage at night, mostly, to avoid desiccation and predation. Some of their subterranean tunnels in the dry season go down fifty feet to the water table. The arboreal termites are more primitive, feeding on the tree to which their great clay globe is fastened.

The other side of the hill overlooked the orderly, tree-lined streets of Sobradinho, and I found a path into a gully with a stream that splashed from rock to rock. Halfway down the gully there was a hovel of scavenged planks and sheetmetal, constructed without the benefit of nails, the roof held down with boulders, the wall elements simply leaned against the roof, a white mule tethered and a banana tree bravely fluttering in the yard, from inside the sound of a child crying, utensils clinking against plates, a shirtless man standing in the doorway. *"Vamos almoçar?"* he hails. My second luncheon invitation of the day. The less people have, it seems, the more generous they are. Below the *casebra* a thin swath of gallery forest escorts the stream into the valley to its meeting with Sobradinho Creek. The trees are tall and straight, encrusted with lichens and cabled with vines, and their canopy is loud with the calls of unseen tanagers and finches, antwrens and antpipits, honeycreepers and woodcreepers. I thread my way among the trees and rocks slowly, vigilant for fer-de-lances. They pose more of a threat to someone who is retracing his path: at first encounter they are usually sprawled out sluggishly, at second coiled and ready. A shack at the bottom of the gully: Adelia Rodriguez Perera, a woman of about fifty, lives here with her children and grandchildren, already ten of them—telescoped generations, telescoped lives. I ask to take their picture. Mrs. Perera goes inside to change her dress. They take their place on a bench against a wall, ranged by age and height. Wide-angle lens necessary to fit them all in. Mrs. Perera, who comes from Minas Gerais, is a firm believer in the curative power of plants, and she shows me the ones in her garden, detailing their uses: "This *piaba* is just for eating, this *orcanfo* is for the heart, and mixed in a tea with this *alikrin*, lowers the blood pressure; a tea brewed from this *trançagem* makes the black spots on your body go away and is also good in salads. Tea of *aruda* brings on menstruation. Tea of Father Nicholas is good for weakness, when the food won't go down into your stomach. Crushed *mastruze* is for dizziness, and boiled in milk, is a vermifuge. There is no kind of worms, even a tapeworm, that it won't flush out. My daughter had one forty meters long. When you have vertigo it means you have worms." Her photograph taken, her pharmacopoeia noted down, I prepare to move on, but am hit up for a third invitation to come in and eat.

———————

When I returned to Brazil this time it was not just as a foreign observer; I had a stake in the culture. Ana and I had been married almost two years. A son, André Luís, had been born a few months earlier, automatically becoming a citizen of both countries. I had thought up his name: André was for a remarkable great-uncle, and I had thrown in the Luís to make it more Latin-sounding. It turned out to be a perfectly respectable name in Brazil; there was even a famous writer and medium, Francis Xavier, who received "psychograms" from a spirit called André Luís. The boy was an instant hit with the in-laws. Dona Joana of course was thrilled to be presented with her first great-grandchild. "Here is a new flower for your garden," I said to her, and taking him into her arms the wise, wrinkled woman wept in gratitude. She had not aged appreciably, having already passed into a timeless senescence when I had first met her, and there was the same measured peacefulness in her voice. Iraci asked if she could raise the boy, "to fill my emptiness." *"Que gracinha!"* the family exclaimed. "How cute!" His nose was pronounced "the spitting image of Tadeu's," while under his left ear he had a mole—the precise location of Paulo's nevus. There was no mistaking that he was a Leonias. Carla Soria, Tété's oldest, christened her little second cousin Travoltinha, after John Travolta, the actor who was the sensation of the moment in Brazil.

While André Luís was already getting his tongue around the
consonants g, v, f, b, p, and d, and producing lengthy
vocalizations whose meaning was only known to him, I had
made strides in my new language, Portuguese. "My God, he
talks like a regular Brazilian, like a country boy from Piauí,"
Tonho exclaimed, realizing that he wouldn't have to use sign
language with me anymore. Having learned five languages
systematically, case ending by irregular verb form, I had tried to
approach Portuguese as unconsciously as possible, as a child
would. I called my method "the niche approach": after you
have heard a word or phrase enough times in a certain situation,
you begin repeating it when that situation crops up again. The
first phrase one inevitably learns is the greeting, *"Tudo bem?"* to
which one may reply *"Tudo bem," "Tudo bom,"* the more pious
"Tudo bom, graças a Deus" ("Everything's fine, praise the Lord"),
or the more urbane *"Tudo bem e nada preste"* ("Everything's fine
and nothing is of any use."). Brazilian Portuguese is full of
ejaculations: *Oi* is uttered at a surprise encounter with a friend,
Puxe is an expression of incredulity, as if the breath has suddenly
been knocked out of you. *Ishi Marie, Opa,* and *Ora Bolas* are other
delightful and important expressions, each with a specific niche.
It is one of the most sensual tongues, reaching in the speech of a
carioca, who pronounces his *s*'s as if they were *sh*'s, the height of
sibilance and sussurance. Perhaps only Russian has a comparable capacity to re-create onomatopoetically, to be forcefully that
of which it is speaking. The Latinate regularity of Portuguese
verb and noun endings makes it an easy language for poets,
while its diminutives and augmentatives make it possible to
achieve shades of expression and ranges of emotion that are
impossible in English. Further, bewitching richness is added by
numerous contributions from the African *bundo* and the native
Tupi-Guarani. Under the letter m, for example, in James L.
Taylor's *A Portuguese-English Dictionary,* one discovers that a
muruxaba (a variant of *murixaba)* is a prostitute, while a

murumuxaua (a variant of *morubixaba)* is a tribal chief or political boss. Not in Taylor is a local Indian term, *murundum.* It refers to the curious mounds that occur in the wet parts of the *cerrado* and for which there is as yet no geological, biological, or anthropological explanation. There are many mysteries in Brazil, and many in Brazilian Portuguese. Take a simple word like skunk. *Cangambá* is the term with the widest currency, but Taylor offers no less than fifteen synonyms or orthographic varients: *iritacaca, iritatataca, jaguane, jaguare, jaguarecaca, jaguarecogua, jaguritaca, jaratataca, jaraticaca, jaritataca, maritacaca, maritafede, marititaca, tacaca,* and *zorrilho.* Some eighty-five indigenous tongues are still spoken in Brazil. In the remote parts of the country Portuguese is often not the principal language, and in the very remote parts a knowledge of Portuguese won't help you at all.

To get along in Brasília it is almost as important to be fluent in another language, the acronymic vocabulary of the bureaucratic and business communities. Every group that forms chooses a sharp-sounding acronym to make itself known to the world. Doormats at the entrance of businesses and institutions are often emblazoned with the cryptic insignia, and without a working command of this second, streamlined language the visitor to modern Brazil and even the backwoods native is sunk. In the library of the Senate I came across a volume called *Brazilian Acronyms.* It was four hundred and thirty-two pages long, with about thirty-five entries per page. BIP was a bureau of private investigation in Recife; FISIBA an outfit that manufactured synthetic fibers in Bahia; FLAFAC the Latin American Federation of Manufacturers of Compound Foods for Animals; OSEMAVI the Socioeducational Organization of the Virgin Santa Marina of São Paulo. Every so often, to confuse matters, several companies would converge on the same acronym. In Curitiba, for example, ESCOL was an engineering firm specializing in soils and concrete; in Rio ESCOL was the Office of Accounting and Authentication; while in Fortaleza ESCOL was a manufacturer of sporting goods. I think my favorite-sounding acronym is CRESSPOM, which I discovered on a sign while driving along the northern rim of Lake Paranoá. CRESSPOM is the Recreational Club of Sublieutenants and Sergeants of the Military Police of the Federal District. Tadeu frequented it when he was on the force. Perched on the sign was almost as exciting a find, a fork-tailed flycatcher. Close relatives of the scissor-tailed flycatchers which grace Texas telephone poles, the fork-tailed flycatchers are highly migratory and have been reported as far north as New Jersey. This one was probably on its way to spend the winter in the Amazon.

Soon after our arrival I met a seasoned observer of life in the capital. His name was Manuel Mendes and he wrote the diplomatic column for the *Correio Brasiliense* besides having an office in the Hotel Nacional, for whom he booked banquets and handled publicity. Mendes was, like Waldemar, a *nordestino* who had come to Brasília early enough to be a *candango* and had started out in the construction yards checking cargo manifests. But Mendes had a special talent for mixing with people, and the sort of presence that brings life to a gathering. He had also written for newspapers since he was seventeen, first in his native state of Paraíba, and later as a freelance in Rio. Soon after the *Correio Brasiliense* was founded Mendes joined its staff. "Since the revolution newspapers in Brazil have been prisoners of the government," he told me. "The journalist hasn't yet been elevated to heroic status as he has in your country, except maybe for the famous Carlos Castelo Branco of the *Jornal do Brasil,* whose courageous outspokenness won several prison sentences. The journalist here has no power. Often his name doesn't even appear with his story. For twelve years, I wrote this column anonymously. Finally, two years ago, they put my name at the bottom. Journalists don't thrive in police states." This conversation took place before censorship of the press was lifted, and gives an idea of how sentiment was running before the *abertura*.

How Mendes found the peace to write was baffling, for every moment the phone in his office would ring, a courier would appear with an engraved invitation from some embassy, Pepe, the hotel's harried manager, would pop in for an urgent consultation, or an old friend would drop by. Mendes seemed at the center of a whirlwind. Liked by many, feared by some, and known to all, he was the man who conferred or withheld status in Brasília. "See Mendes," an officer at the American Embassy had told me. "He keeps up the pretense that this is a brilliant social scene. Ask him who the big hosts in town are. Most of them are the ambassadors of small and very interesting countries. Since they have relatively little to do that is substantive, they do a lot of entertaining. Their job is to spread the word, to make themselves and thus their countries liked."

Unlike his counterparts in Rio, who hardly even referred to a happening in Brasília except derisively, Mendes managed almost always to be positive. "I usually give a straight account of who was there," he explained, "naming the prominent and what they had on. This is a closed society and my paper is very conservative. But every so often something flagrant happens—like the ambassador of Mexico a few years back: he was a heavy drinker, didn't pay his debts, and had a wife who kept leaving receptions with other men." Physically Mendes was small, with the characteristic *cabeça chata* or flat head of the *nordestino*. (A standing joke in Brazil explains that every youngster in the Northeast has a flat head because his father keeps patting it and saying, "My boy when he grows up will be president.") His face was always lit with good cheer and his lips pursed in a smile, and his eyes missed nothing.

He made his rounds in an off-white Chevrolet Impala from that period when American cars were built like cabin cruisers. It was one of the largest automobiles in the capital. "This city has had its highs and lows," he said one evening as we were cruising toward the residence of the ambassador of the Ivory Coast. "The most nervous point was during the first six months after the revolution. No one was sure what the government would do. The capital was incomplete. Many of the ministries were still in Rio. But in the end they decided to occupy it, in spite of Niemeyer's politics. When I came here in 1957 there were only two classes—the engineers and the workers. The engineers were allowed to have their families, and the first social manifestations were gatherings in their compounds—dinners, birthday parties, dances to the Victrola. After the inauguration came the clubs, which are still important. The most prestigious is the Yacht Club, where the young and beautiful hang out—you know, those pretty things who lie around in *tanginhas,* minimal bikinis. We used to go waterskiing at the Yacht Club. Now the lake is too polluted.

"In 1961 the Hotel Nacional opened. It was immense—the largest hotel in South America. I think it's still the third or fourth largest. It soon became the center of chic society. Maria Teresa, João Goulart's wife, was *muito alegre,* and she was the queen of the black-tie nights at the Hotel Nacional. Big-name singers started playing the hotel, and a woman who had read Tolstoy's *Resurrection* began to call herself Katusha and to write a society column in the *Correio Brasiliense.* Then the military took over, and an invitation to one of the service clubs was suddenly the most sought-after thing in Brasília. Large ceremonial functions, like the recent reception for the president of France at the Naval Club, are still held in the service clubs. During the regimes of Castelo Branco and Costa e Silva white tie was in

145

effect. The great event of the white-tie era was a gigantic reception in 1969 for the shah of Iran. Coarse, uncultured *empresários* and deputies from the interior—people who had never traveled—showed up in colorful mixtures of black and white tie. It was a ridiculous occasion. The columnists in Rio called it 'diplomacy from the backlands.'"

We crossed the Costa e Silva Bridge, one of Brasília's architectural wonders. The completion of its five-hundred-foot free span, the greatest of any nonsuspension bridge in Latin America, gave more trouble than any other Niemeyer project. Technical problems extended the construction time from two to six years. During the insertion of its keystone, television cameras were trained on it night and day, waiting for it to fall into the lake. It didn't. We had now left the Plano and were in the South Lake Mansion Sector. The vegetation was mostly juvenile eucalyptus, with round, blue, perfoliate leaves. The architecture was basic Santa Barbara—white stucco walls and vermilion tile roofs—with a degree of self-indulgence that would probably have angered Niemeyer. Those who lived here were either rich or had a foreign government behind them.

"In 1970," Manuel continued, "with the construction of Itamarati Palace and the transfer of the State Department, the social life of the capital became more elevated. Diplomats who had been used to receptions in Paris and Washington started to entertain, and there was a new frequency of parties, at which champagne, whiskey, and French wine flowed freely, since the embassies were exempt from import tax. There are five types of gathering. The *vin d'honneur* is given on the occasion of a country's national day. It takes place at midday and is for men only. In the beginning, there was some confusion because the Brazilians brought their wives. Now they know better."

"The celebration of Yemen's independence that we went to last week at the Aeronautics Club—that must have been a *vin d'honneur,* no?"

"*Claro.* You noticed that there were no women and all the major ambassadors were present. Yemen is an important place these days."

"I was startled by the fact that the ambassadors of West Germany and the Soviet were conversing in English. English must be the lingua franca of diplomacy, as it is of scientific symposia and airport control towers."

"*Claro.* And you noticed that everyone—except you—was wearing a dark suit. The second type of gathering—the cocktail party—begins at 6:30 and is usually over quickly. We are going to a cocktail party. The ambassador of the Ivory Coast, Charles Gomis, is one of Brasília's most active hosts. The party is in honor of Karlos Rischbieter, the president of the Bank of Brazil, who is about to become the new minister of finance. There will be a lot of bankers. It will be a good opportunity to get a *papagaio.*" (A *papagaio,* literally a parrot, means a loan in Brazilian slang.)

"The third category—the reception—differs from the cocktail party in that it starts at eight and has more food. At a buffet reception—the fourth kind—you sit and eat, choosing your table and dinner partners. At a seated dinner—the last type—the dress is almost always black tie and the hostess arranges the seating. There are two seating systems: in the French system, the host and hostess sit at either end of the table with the guests of honor at their left and right hands; the American system has the host, hostess, and guests of honor at the middle of the table, with everyone else trailing off in diminishing importance. Depending on what sort of gathering it is, you receive one of three types of invitations. *Vins d'honneur* and cocktail parties are usually 'regrets only.' Receptions and buffet receptions are invariably 'r.s.v.p.,' and for a seated dinner the 'r.s.v.p.' is followed, some fifteen days later, by a 'p.m.,' a *pour memoir* to remind you that you were consulted before and accepted. In the beginning, when seated dinners began to be given in Brasília,

147

there was a lot of confusion. The Brazilians never answered—
you know how vague we can be about such things—or they
accepted and never came, or they came several hours late
and brought all their friends, or they came on time but during the preliminary drinks switched around the place cards
and sat next to the new friends they had made. The embassies
fumed. To this day you still don't know if a deputy will show
up or if he will come with his friends. The no-shows are doubly
embarrassing because the missing guest's place card is in plain
view and it is too late for the hostess to shrink the size of
the table or to find a replacement. As a result, because there
aren't many Brazilians on their level here, who understand
the protocol, the diplomats tend to socialize among themselves.
You end up seeing the same faces again and again. Those
who were used to Rio complain of the monotony, but when
you take away the social life of the diplomats," he shrugged,
"what is left?"

The ambassador's residence was at the end of a shady cul-de-
sac and screened from view by a dense hedge. It was a
sumptuous modern house with a pool and a patio on which forty
or so dark-suited men were already gathered. As might have
been expected, a lot of ivory was in evidence. Raw tusks guarded
doorways, carved ivory elephants and busts of regal African
women took up coffee tables. The ambassador and his wife were
at the door, receiving guests. He was a poised and ingratiating
man of thirty-eight and she, in a long gown, "was as stunning as
a model," Manuel would report in next morning's paper. Most
of the guests were clustered around Mr. Rischbieter, who, as
flashbulbs popped around him, was dropping guarded pearls
about the economy. Ten ambassadors were in attendance. I met
those from Switzerland, India, Syria, Egypt, and Morocco, none
of whose country's relations with Brazil were of any great importance. "What are you doing here in Brazil?" I asked the Swiss
ambassador. "Nothing," he answered affably. The ambassador

148

of India had a white turban and beard. "The Indian presence in Brazil is slight," he explained. "We are a mere fifteen hundred, with neither the problems of Indians in South Africa and Great Britain, nor the success story of the Indians in the United States." Conspicuous by their absence were the Americans. Manuel said he hardly ever saw them at receptions and couldn't remember when he'd last been invited to the American Embassy. "Although they invented the science of public relations, they seem to have stopped practicing it."

The Afro-Brazilian connection, on the other hand, seemed to be strengthening by the minute. This was understandable, considering the natural affinities of the two continents, the close parallels of vegetation, geology, climate, racial stock, and economic status. Even the Brazilian flag, though its pattern is Masonic, has typical African colors: blue, yellow, and green. Africa, moreover, is the nearest land mass. It is four hours from Brasília to Abidjan, the capital of the Ivory Coast. In fact Mr. Rischbieter would be flying to Abidjan in a few days to open a new branch of the Bank of Brazil; there would be a week-long celebration of the two countries' rapprochement, climaxed with a concert by the famous Brazilian singer Clara Nunes. "As you know, banks never go in places where they have no interest," Mr. Gomis said to me in perfect English; he had gotten a masters degree from UCLA. Thereupon he recited his country's vital statistics: number one world producer of cacão this year, number two in palm oil, number three in coffee, number one in Africa for bananas, timber, and pineapples; highest per capita income in black Africa (seven hundred dollars per annum); population, seven million; area, six times that of the Federal District; techniques for synthesizing soap and perfume from palm oil so advanced that "I don't know if we should reveal them." The embassy in Brasília, he said, was one of his country's most important. "It is not a spy embassy, like some of the others. We are here because we want to do business.

Because our countries have so much in common culturally and ecologically, because they have both gone through underdevelopment and are now at *décollage,* or 'takeoff,' as you would call it, it makes sense that they should turn to each other. It makes more sense for the Ivory Coast, for example, to buy a simple, solid tractor from Brazil than a delicate, sophisticated one from West Germany. The Brazilian tractor is, basically, the American tractor of 1947, adapted to the soil and climate of the Amazon. If it breaks down any man can repair it. The German tractor is equipped with air conditioning, but when it breaks down a hundred miles from Abidjan, only an engineer from MIT will know how to fix it. And Brazil understands that when she sells us fifty tractors, she will send us five or six technicians who will show our people how to run them and will help build a factory of which Brazil will be part owner. Brazil's new industry is looking for markets abroad, and we are embarking on many joint ventures. And it's easier doing business with Brazil because there is no colonial taste in our dealings. It's not a North-South relationship. We can treat each other as equals."

Manuel and I continued to the French Embassy, arriving in time to watch the ambassador tie a decoration around the neck of a deserving Brazilian admiral and buss him once on either cheek. The Embassy was attractive but stuffy; whoever designed it had not paid enough attention to its ventilation. The French, who, after all, were responsible for most of the protocol which diplomats are obliged to observe, were also stuffy. A haughty young attaché, after listening to my·French for several minutes, announced brusquely *"Je ne peux plus,"* and turned away. The number two man, recently arrived, was nicer. "Brasília is a demi-success," he said. "It has no *âme*. Why didn't Kubitschek build the capital in Diamantina, his birthplace—a lovely old town?" We waited for Ana, who was to meet us there, and as soon as she arrived, proceeded to a military reception at the residence of the ambassador of Peru. While Manuel darted deftly among brocaded and epauleted Latin American military attachés, Ana sat with their wives, and I struck up a conversation with the ambassador. Having just read how the citizens of Cuzco had been tearing up the streets and hurling the cobblestones at passing cars in protest of the latest devaluation of the sol, I asked him how the situation was. "We were up to here," he said, bringing his hand level with his nose. "Now we're up to here," he said, and lowered it to his chin. Then he spoke of "heavy vibrations" he'd been getting from the ancient spirits of the Planalto—"This is one of the oldest places on earth, you know." In the sitting room, while the men were discussing subjects vital to national security, their wives were wearing Cheshire cat smiles and prattling obliviously.

"We have more money than we know what to do with, my Jorgito and I," one was saying, "but I'm not *realizada*. Perhaps I should set up a business of my own. What about a tourist agency? My mother-in-law recently took a group tour in Manaus and had a wonderful time."

"Out of the question," her friend retorted. "There are twenty-five agencies already. Five are active and the others aren't worth a damn. Besides, everyone knows there's no tourism in Brasília. You can see what there is to see in a day. And think how boring it would be, trucking around those busloads of tourists. People who choose to travel together in guided tours have no *personalidade,* no minds of their own."

"Then what about a boutique?"

"Even more stupid. You know how quickly boutiques go under, even with the best merchandise. A lot of people come in and try things on, but at the end of the day, how many sales have you rung up?"

One of the women was the famous Katusha. She was still writing her column, but after almost twenty years it had lost much of its punch and much of its clout. Having chronicled the scene from its incipience, she had become a part of it. I asked her what the lives of socially prominent women in Brasília consisted of. "Dinners, receptions, cocktails at the embassies," she said wearily. "Art shows and autographing parties at the hotels. Fashion shows at the clubs. Cards at each other's houses in the afternoon. Everyone plays *biriba,* which is like gin rummy."

Manuel had been invited to dinner by the Syrian ambassador and we had not so we parted company, and getting into the Variant, Ana and I headed back across the Costa e Sliva Bridge to 109 South, where there are a number of good Arab restaurants. 109 South is the Bleecker Street, the King's Road, the boulevard St.-Michel of Brasília, the meeting place of a growing number of artists, intellectuals, homosexuals, pot-smokers, and undercover agents. In front of the Beirute, the best-known of the restaurants, several dozen motorcycles were parked, and young bikers were constantly pulling in or out of the lineup. Taking an outdoor table, we were soon accosted by a former colleague of Ana's at FUNAI who had kept getting medical excuses from work until he was finally fired. Soon afterward, Ana had heard, he was busted for possession of marijuana, and as he sat with us it was obvious from his languid lids and the remoteness of his speech that he still smoked regularly. We spoke about FUNAI and the Indians. The Xavante, whose distrust of white men was longstanding, had lately developed a new militancy that resembled the "red power" movement of our native Americans. Several of their *toushauas,* or tribal leaders, had become sufficiently acculturated to manipulate the media into helping create a more favorable political climate for the Indian. A few months before they had appeared at the Planalto Palace and demanded an audience with the president. "I'm sorry," an aide had told them, "you can't see him without a tie." The *toushauas* had immediately called a press conference and announced that no *civilizado* would be allowed into a Xavante village without the proper ceremonial headdress. Recently the Xavante had voted down a government proposal to make them full citizens of Brazil when they realized that in the process they would lose title to their lands, which they had been granted as wards of the state. The Indians' territory and their way of life was as vulnerable as ever. Only that morning a woman at FUNAI had been exposed for selling Negative Certificates, meaning that a certain piece of land did not belong to the Indians and could therefore be settled—when she knew perfectly well that the property in question was part of a *reserva indígena*. Someone posing as a farmer had made a tape of the transaction and sold it to the newspapers.

The former colleague left us, and the waiter brought on steamy platters of couscous and curry—more than two of us could possibly eat. Three shoeshine boys came to our table. There are about twenty-five thousand abandoned children in the District, and between thirteen and fourteen million in Brazil at large, a specialist on the problem told us. Fifty-one percent of the population is under nineteen. "Of all the children in the first grade, only 40 percent finish the fifth," he said. "Malnutrition is the reason for the 60 percent dropout rate. Most of their brain cells are knocked out before they're five. Lethargy sets in. It's not correctible." The urchins, or *pivetes,* of Brasília are not as aggressive as the ones in Rio, who will steal food off your plate when you're not looking. They offer to mind your car or to wash it, to show you the city or shine your shoes. The three boys were like irresistible puppies, too polite to beg. "You hungry?" I asked. They nodded in unison. "Then *vamos comer,"* I said. The waiter threw up his arms when I asked for three more plates, and the people at the other tables turned and nodded approvingly, several even raising their glasses, as the boys sat down and started shoveling in the food. I told them they didn't have to eat so quickly. "Don't worry, I'm not going to change my mind."

"What's your name?" Ana asked the oldest, who was thirteen.

"André Luís Rodriguez."

"That's a nice name," she said. "Our son is called André Luís." The other two were brothers, Antonio and José Brasil Alves de Freitas. André Luís had an aunt in Sobradinho, and the de Freitas brothers came from Gama. They were all on vacation and had met at the Plano, where they had gone to make some money. They gave about ten shines a day, at ten cruzeiros each, and at night slept in a nearby cinema. "I came to live with my aunt six months ago," André Luís told us. "My mother lives in Minas Gerais. My father left her when I was little. She didn't know how to take care of me so she gave me to her sister."

"Are you Portuguese?" he asked some time later. I had ordered a shine, and he was scrubbing the red dirt from the edges of my shoes with a toothbrush.

"No, American."

The youngest brother, José Brasil, got up the courage to ask a question. "Do you know Wonder Woman?"

"Claro."

"She exists, or is she just a story?"

"She exists."

"Come on," Antonio said. "You think she really fights off those bullets?"

In a capital that was built as a showpiece, it is understandable that the Ministry of Foreign Relations, being responsible for the nation's appearance to the world, should get the most handsome edifice. The Itamarati Palace is Niemeyer's masterwork in Brasília, and one of the world's most serenely lyrical public buildings—a low-slung structure sitting in water and accessible only by ramps, with an outer sheath of tall, slender arches enclosing and shading its glass sides. The arches, of laminated concrete that is grey and finely pockmarked with a decade's weathering, are a stylization of Brazilian colonial architecture; they recall, too, the vaulted Palace of Justice which

Le Corbusier had created for Chandigarh, the new capital of Punjab, in 1953. Rising out of the water, their tranquil spans bound symmetrically to the horizon with the final arch at each corner of the building somewhat enlarged to correct the diminishing effect of perspective. Islands of fantastic vegetation, to which the gardeners pole a small aluminum boat, float in the lake, and within the arches, at one end, the building was left open, its great central hall shielded by two-story stands of climbing philodendron. The plants were put there by Robert Burle-Marx, the great Brazilian landscape architect. Burle-Marx, who is also a highly regarded abstract painter, belongs to the same wave of creativity in Rio that produced Niemeyer and Lúcio Costa. He got his start, in fact, when Costa, his neighbor in the thirties, admired his garden and asked if he would do one for *him*. This led to his being entrusted with larger gardens in Brazil, public and private, and eventually the municipal parks of Hamburg and Vienna. "The landscape gardener in Brazil is free to build gardens from the floral reality of an overwhelming richness," he said one morning as we sat on the veranda of his two-hundred-acre *sítio* on a mountaintop south of Rio. "Nowhere are there so many vegetal associations—five thousand arboreal species at our disposal alone." Burle-Marx is the most vocal champion of his country's native flora. "It is not that I am chauvinistic," he explained, "but it is so important that we understand all that is here. I would like to show you my collection, based on a great many expeditions throughout Brazil. Four hundred fifty species of philodendron . . . one of the greatest collections of heliconia in the world. . . ." Burle-Marx was not in on the general planning of Brasília because of a difference with Juscelino, but when the buildings were finished, he was invited to landscape them and to lay out a botanical garden with plants representative of the ecological regions in Brazil. "I wanted to have a forest like that of Amazonia, but it was impossible with the climatic conditions of the plateau, with its six months of dryness. Only hemicryptophytous vegetation, trees ten feet tall with thirty-foot root systems, grow in the *cerrado*. I think those twisted little trees are a *maravilha*. A tree, after all, is not there to please us. It has its own biological life." So Burle-Marx abandoned the dream of a Hyde Park or a Bois de Boulogne in Brasília—the irrigation would have been prohibited—and concentrated on aquatic gardens and skylit building-interior gardens. He landscaped the Congress, the American Embassy, the fountains at Rogerio Pithon Farias Park. But his triumph was the Itamarati Palace: not only did he embellish it with plant arrangements that were like vegetable sculptures, but he drew cartoons for the massive tapestries on the third floor, where the inaugural ball is held, where new ambassadors present their credentials on Monday mornings, where state functions of the highest importance are given.

Every morning at ten or so a black Mercedes limousine stops at a plated metal wall at the rear of the palace. The wall rises by remote control and the limousine continues up a ramp to the second floor, where it stops. Out steps the secretary general, the number two man in the Ministry of Foreign Relations. From there he has about a thirty-foot walk to his office. The secretary general in the closing days of Geisel's presidency was a shrewd, highly cultured diplomat named Dario Moreira de Castro Alves. Ambassador Dario, I discovered on the morning I called on him, was no taller than Manuel Mendes and wore his grey hair in a rigid crewcut. He was sitting behind a huge desk and sifting through the morning's stack of printed matter—interoffice memos, confidential reports, foreign newspapers. I began by saying that in a country where sweetness and civility were so much a part of the national character, there must be a strong diplomatic tradition. "Yes," he said. "Brazil has a deep sediment of diplomatic habit because we have ten neighbors with whom to settle our limits." The ambassador's English was excellent. "Only the Soviet Union has more neighbors, thirteen or fourteen, I think." It was admirable, I said, how Brazil managed to keep good relations with each of them, while they seemed always to be involved in border skirmishes among each other. Few countries have had such a placid history, at least externally. Was it that Brazil is so big that the other countries on the continent didn't dare to pick a fight with it? Or was it the contentment of its people, who wanted nothing more than what they had already and seemed incapable of imperialistic behavior?

"I think it has to do with the difference between the Spanish and the Portuguese," Ambassador Dario said. "The Portuguese *torero* does not kill the bull. Ever since the second half of the eighteenth century, when the son of King Dom José was killed in a bullfight, there has been no killing of the bull. The Spanish are more *sanguinário*, more bloodthirsty. And the Portuguese, being already used to Moors in their midst, were more tolerant and socially mobile. It is revealing, I think, that the Portuguese settlement was preserved in a single block, while the Spanish settlement was broken up into small, volatile republics. Even our internal disorders are seldom violent. Agreed, the Civil War of 1930 was rather nasty, but all our coups d'etat since then, those in 1937, 1945, and, 1964, have been bloodless."

The only regrettable side effect of the lack of belligerence in Brazil, I suggested, was that it, plus the fact that the country is on the tectonically quiet side of the continent, seemed to have doomed Brazil to utter neglect by the North American press. How, I asked, had the Itamarati Palace gotten its name?

"Itamarati is a Tupi-Guarani word meaning 'white rock,'" he said. "There are hundreds of rivers, islands, and streams with that name. It is common in Amazonian toponymics, and was, in the days of the Empire, a noble title. The first Baron of Itamarati, José Joaquim da Rocha, built a beautiful Italian neoclassical house in Rio near the Praça da República. It was called the House and later the Palace of the Baron of Itamarati.

In 1890, one year after the Republic was proclaimed, the palace was bought by the government and served as the headquarters of the president while the Palace of Catete was being constructed. In 1899 it was rented to the Ministry of Foreign Relations. Three years later the Baron of Rio Branco, our most illustrious foreign minister, occupied it, and since then the word Itamarati has been associated with Brazilian diplomacy. One of President Castelo Branco's last decrees, in March 1967, was that the official name of the new headquarters of the Ministry of Foreign Relations in Brasília be called not the Palace of the Arches, as originally proposed, but the Itamarati Palace."

He spoke of the stages of Brazil's economic growth. The sixteenth century had been dedicated to the extraction of brazilwood; the seventeenth to sugar; the eighteenth to gold and diamond mining; the nineteenth to coffee; the beginning of the twentieth to rubber. "Now we are in a period of diversification, of polyculture and heavy industrialization. And in the transfer of technology from the developed nations—IBM, Olivetti, Japanese electronics, West German atomic power—Itamarati is the conductor. Unlike the Latin American countries with a high Indian population, such as Mexico and Peru, we have no cultural barriers against the importation of progress, and our clergy is not reactionary as it was in Russia, though if Islam becomes too important a temporal force in the Middle East, I'm worried it may influence the progressive Catholic Church in Latin America. Our big task is to build the economy. But we must spread its base, too, or as in the Soviet Union it will be too compressed. On the other hand, if you share too much of your wealth before building, as in Uruguay the cake you share will be poverty. The condition of reaching the optimum point of sharing and building defines statesmanship. We are now passing France to become the number two world exporter of food. This is important in a world that will be more and more hungry not only because of the increase of population but because people's consumer capacity will rise as urbanization spreads and more and more are affected by progress. Of the five big countries, Brazil is the most adaptable to agriculture. It has no great mountains, deserts, or frozen wastes, and 80 percent of its area can easily be farmed." The figure seemed high, but I did not question it.

I noticed how many times the ambassador had mentioned Russia as a measure of comparison with his own country. The similarities between the two countries are intriguing: both are immense, with vast areas of intractable wilderness, Siberia and Amazonia. Both have large segments of unassimilated non-Europeans in their populations. Their "soul" is not quite European, and this is important to understand. In both there has been (I am speaking now of prerevolutionary Russia) a tremendous disparity between the rich and the poor, and a highly stratified social order, with patient, illiterate masses at the bottom; the "Russian attitude of resignation toward an autocratic regime," of which Toynbee wrote, is also a Brazilian trait. Both wallow in florid, runaway bureaucracies, and in both the role of the miraculous and the supernatural is of great importance—one can think of Arigo, the Brazilian peasant who, until his death in 1971, astounded the medical profession with his feats of surgery and healing, as a latter-day and more benign Rasputin.

Ambassador Dario was prone to think of his country in terms of Russia because, under Khrushchev, he had been ambassador there. In a matter of a few weeks, when President Geisel stepped down, he was going abroad again, this time as the ambassador to Portugal, a post that was regarded as the plum of Brazil's foreign service, and was awarded only to trusted senior diplomats.

"I'm so happy Dario is being sent to Portugal," said his wife, the celebrated novelist Dinah Silveira de Queiroz. She is one of Brasília's *grandes dames,* the sort of woman whose hand it seems appropriate to seize and kiss. In the absence of an indigenous aristocracy, which takes years to evolve, Dona Dinah was the only person in Brasília whom I would have instantly placed in the upper class. She was a tall, patrician woman of about sixty. "I am descended from *bandeirantes* who came to Brazil in the beginning of the seventeenth century," she said. "My ancestor, Carlos Pedro de Silveira, minted the first gold money. He appears in my novel, *A Muralha*, The Rampart." Her house, on the Peninsula of Ministers, a compound on the lake's southern rim for prominent members of government, was called the Vila Muralha after her most famous novel. It was built in 1969, when her husband was called from Italy to help in the transfer of Itamarati to Brasília; but surrounded with an outer brick wall—a rampart—with small circular windows, it seemed to have been there much longer. "In those days, the women stayed home and minded the *fazenda*," she went on. "The men passed sometimes years away, prospecting. When they came home they brought their 'children of the woods,' their offspring with Indian women. That was the beginning of miscegenation. Today the youth of Brazil is one of the most beautiful on earth. We are a country of *mestiços*. But each year Brazil is becoming whiter. It was always thought that the black genes were stronger and would prevail, but this is not proving the case. Only ten million of us are still pure black." Dona Dinah had received me in her library, wearing a long red gown with a lace border. Her fingers were encrusted with rings. Touching on this and that, she spoke in a vague, decelerated drawl, that gave her time to study her listeners. Her library, which took up the walls of several rooms, was undoubtedly the largest private one in Brasília, and it gave off a pleasant smell of old leather. Some of the books had been her father's. She showed his Baedecker guide to Egypt and the first volume of the encyclopedia he had been writing when he died. His encyclopedia had promised to rival the Britannica, but he had only managed to complete the letter A. One wall was devoted to her own works. *A Muralha* was about the first nationalistic stirrings in Brazil. It had been translated into Russian and Japanese and been the basis of a soap opera. *The Summer of the Infidels* was a *nouveau roman* whose action had been compressed into three days. *Margarida la Rogue* was "the phantasm of a woman on a desert island, a Proustian meditation on the feminine condition." Two novels about the life of Jesus had been written in Brasília. "I had many doubts about being able to write about Christ in the first person, but Pope Paul the VI wrote me a letter of congratulation, and the books have been translated into Hebrew." She opened a cabinet whose shelves bulged with notebooks and manila envelopes. "My diaries. I have been making daily entries for forty years. I would have more than a hundred books if I published them." On the next wall were Dario's books about political science and Brazilian history. "The diplomacy of Brazil is one of the most perfect in the world," she said. "Unlike American ambassadors, who are often friends of politicians, ours receive rigorous training. The hierarchy of diplomacy here is like that of the Church. But as yet there are few women or blacks in the foreign service. The first black woman to reach a high diplomatic post, who beat out all the men in the *concursos,* was named Monica. I invited her to tea, having written an article called 'I'm Going to Invite Monica to Tea.' She cried." Dona Dinah wrote a weekly column about cultural affairs for the *Correio Brasiliense* and had been conducting a radio monologue called "Morning Coffee," "a humanitarian commentary on daily happenings," for thirty years. She was president of the Academy of Brasília and "the most expressive cultural figure in the capital," according to Manuel Mendes, for whose forthcoming memoir, *Testimony to Brasília,* she had written an introduction. "This library is much visited by writers," she said. "I am trying to create a tradition of culture in Brasília. Our proudest achievement, the greatest thing that has ever happened for our national morale, is this city. It was built by people from the Brazilian backlands. When I think how the *candangos* could erect something as exquisite as the Itamarati Palace, I am filled with pride."

Leading me to the rare book section, she took down several incunabula, an early deluxe edition of Byron with hand-painted illustrations, a tall book called *The Dance of the Brazilian Indians,* with superb engravings of their feather art and body-painting. "In *A Muralha* I recounted the early barbarities. It's still hard for the Indians. They lose their culture faster here than in Central America. But I am opposed to keeping them in zoos. I think we have an obligation to develop the human being to the maximum. Today we are the first of the undeveloped countries. Our territory is so great that we can have flooding in the North and drought in the South, as is presently happening. We have many riches but they are unevenly distributed. We are in the place that Europe was many years ago, where many are suffering for progress. We are paying tribute for our difference with the developed world, suffering what a whole class in Europe went through in the nineteenth century—children working in factories, so many dying of consumption—to reach industrialization."

I admired the sweep and the candor of Dinah's thinking, and visited her several times. We exchanged our books, and I told her some of my Indian stories. On my farewell visit she presented me with a gaucho knife from Rio Grande do Sul. Clenching a piece of meat in one's teeth, one was meant to cut off a manageable chunk of it. Its handle and scabbard were of finely tooled pewter. A scene embossed on the scabbard showed a gaucho lassoing a bull, with three copses of majestic *araucária* trees in the background. The knife belonged to Dinah's collection of daggers and letter openers. She also collected matchbooks and animal figurines, and had brought back a fine collection of icons from Russia. When I turned to her column in the *Correio Brasiliense* a few days later, I realized that she had also collected me. The article was about a young American writer named Malcolm Silverman who had come to see her. After describing a book he had produced on Brazilian literature, she proceeded to have Silverman recount one of my Indian stories. I never learned whether she had forgotten whom she had heard the story from, or whether her article was simply a collage of the young men who had recently come to pay her homage.

The richest man in Brasília, Antonio Venâncio da Silva, started as a drover in Ceará, hauling coffee, *farinha,* and sinuous gourds filled with cane juice to market on the backs of mules. A driving man of action, he never found time to master the printed page. To this day reading is a chore for him, and he prefers to leave the paperwork to his trusted secretary, Elza, and to José Nicodemos, his son and the heir apparent of his empire. Eventually, Venâncio traded in his pack animals for a truck. By 1953 he was flourishing in Rio as an exporter of coffee, and had put up seven high-rise buildings in Copacabana and Leblon. In 1959 the coffee crop was a record breaker, and Venâncio celebrated with a trip abroad. He was in New York on May 18, 1960, when news he was waiting for reached him: Brasília had been opened to private enterprise. "I dropped everything and came home," he told me in his office at Venâncio 2000, his second massive shopping complex in the capital and the current titleholder for the largest commercial edifice in Latin America. "Today all Brazil accepts and believes in Brasília," he said. "But it wasn't like that in the beginning. I was one of the first believers. The greatest *pioneiro* in Brasília was me," he said, poking my shoulder for emphasis. "Juscelino came to my house a year before he died. We had never met. He had seen my buildings and wanted to meet me. After dinner I remember he took off his shoes and made a toast:

Viva o maior candango de Brasília. Give me ten men like Venâncio and I wouldn't have built the capital in three years—it would have gone much faster.'" Venâncio's enterprises in Brasília did not start to take off until after the revolution, when there were no strikes to impede construction. He was in the business of erecting commercial houses and renting out their space. His first effort, Edifício Venâncio, the twin of the Conjunto Nacional in the Sector of Diversions, was enormously successful. In 1977 he built Venâncio 2000. "I have traveled," he said, taking me into its hallway, "and there is no more luxurious house of commerce that exists." The tenants of its nine floors, three of which were below ground, included banks, pizzarias, airlines, boutiques, tourist agencies, and public organs like the Ministry of Agriculture. Two floors were taken up with his own Casa da Banha, a department store that carried such imported novelties as bicycles, tents, and styrofoam surfboards. "Camping is just hitting the District," he explained, "and the surfboards were for use in the wavemaking pool which had just been installed in Rogerio Pithon Farias Park at a cost of over a million dollars. "Look at this," he said, leading me into a room where there was a scale model of an even more epic edifice, Venâncio 2001. Scheduled for completion by April 21, 1981, the twenty-first anniversary of Brasília, it would take up three blocks and have twelve stories, four of which were subterranean because the skyline in that part of the city was not allowed to exceed eight stories. Its architecture was that of the other Venâncios, bedizened 1940s. Obviously, the man was indefatigable. Though he professed to have retired years ago he was still very much present, hovering over the operation. "In my leisure, I think of work," he said. "When I'm traveling, I'm always reaching for a phone to find out what's happening." Dark-complexioned, his shirt open with a medallion and chain from his store around his neck, he seemed like a virile fifty-year-old. He was, in reality, sixty-seven. "I have the greatest fortune in Brasília, so they say," he said. One newspaper story credited him with owning a third of the real estate in the capital, where "he reigns without a trace of arrogance or conceit." Venâncio was the king of the city's *empresários*.

He was so touched by my interest in him that he invited me to his house for lunch a few days later. The house, in the South Lake Mansion Sector, was a *caixote* the size of a small pyramid, with two second-story verandas, each big enough to accommodate a dozen Casa da Banha patio chairs. The living room was large enough to hold four living room ensembles of three armchairs, a sofa, and a coffee table apiece. Heavy arras with brocaded cords blotted out the sunlight. Imported crystal chandeliers with pendant blue halfmoons dangled from the ceilings. Bucolic tapestries with scenes of eighteenth-century France covered the walls. We sat in one of the ensembles—he, Elza, José Nicodemos, and I. They seemed to be monitoring him nervously, to make sure he didn't say anything off color. A bottle of Johnnie Walker Red Label was produced in my honor. "In the United States, you had Rockefeller and Lincoln who rose from nothing," he said. "Everybody wanted to know how they did it. But here nobody cares. Nobody asks Venâncio the formula of his success." He shrugged. "Well I'll give it to you: a lot of vision and a lot of work. I always investigate a deal before entering it, but when I enter, it is always with enthusiasm and optimism. Like Juscelino. If he had been like the other presidents, it would have taken him fifty years to build the capital. And another thing: I've never had to advertise in the papers for workers. They always came to me. Because I was one of them," he said, jabbing me in the shoulder just as I was about to take a sip of scotch. Lunch was rice and beans with *farinha*, meat and tomatoes; success had not spoiled his taste for simple food. Afterward we toured the house. He showed me his bed, with its built-in television and tape deck, his bathroom, which was vast enough to have its own garden, and the three rooms of his children, who were at school in Switzerland.

———————

"Brasília's like a garden that's just been planted," a friend in Rio observed. "It has no character. That'll take a century." What that character will be is difficult to say, except that it will belong to the nonregional, pan-Brazilian future. The first crop of native *candangos* are coming of age; Brasílio Franklin de Queiroz, the first baby born in Brasília (on March 30, 1957), is already in his twenties. It is said that only when *their* children have grown up will a recognizable structure have settled on life in Brasília, and a distinct personality have emerged. That this personality will not be solely bureaucratic is suggested by the number of artists who have already moved to the District, attracted to the majesty of the plateau. Among them are the nationally known poet, Domingos Carvalho da Silva; the musician Waldir Azevedo, who is to the *cavaquinho* what Bill Munroe is to the mandolin; and the painter Milton Ribeiro. Ribeiro lives in the North Lake Mansion Sector, fifteen minutes from the Plano. The houses there are smaller and less showy than in the South Lake Mansion Sector. Many lots are still open *cerrado*, and many are under construction. Ribeiro's *caixote* is strikingly landscaped. He had the intelligence to leave many of the original trees standing; his was the only yard I saw in Brasília in which the *cerrado* had not been completely razed and replaced with exotic plantings. "The people who come to live here don't realize the beauty of the trees," Ribeiro said. "But for me the whole *cerrado* is a garden. When I saw the anguished deformity of the trees, it

166

had great connotation for me. As you can see, twisted trees keep appearing in my work. To me they are like the suffering people of the world." We walked among his trees: a lantern tree, a holy-wood tree, an earpod tree, a tapir's toenail tree, whose bark, pulverized and inhaled, was said to be good for a runny nose, an orange tabernaemontana tree, which made some who approached it start to itch. "I wonder what Van Gogh would have thought," I said, "if he had known that trees very much the way he painted them really existed?"

"I try to transport everything from the landscape of Brasília into my art," he went on—"its amplitude and light, its predominance of the horizontal, which in graphic language is characteristic of tranquility; its tonalities: the hot reds and browns of its earth, the greens of its trees, the carmine pour of its sun—the whole visual impregnation." Ribeiro had grown up in Jacaré Paguá, a rural suburb of Rio, the grandson of a slave and the son of a Portuguese. He was a strong-featured man, with wavy grey hair, coffee-colored skin, and penetrating blue eyes. At an early age he had, without anyone's encouragement, begun to copy the illustrations in newspapers and magazines. Rising in the artistic circles of Rio, he got to know Burle-Marx and fell under the spell, especially, of the expressionist Cândido Portinari. In 1967 he accepted a position at the University of Brasília as a professor of graphics and visual communication. His work had been exhibited in Paris, and he had recently mounted a one-man show in the Itamarati Palace. Ribeiro painted in three styles. "The Flagelados," a large canvas showing a huddle of drought victims from the Northeast arranged like a grotesquely twisted *cerrado* tree, was expressionistic. This mode was reserved for forceful social messages, like the portrait of a sallow, emaciated child he was completing as his statement for the International Year of the Child. "This is my cry of alert for humanity," he said. In a mode which he called geometric constructivism, he painted soft-colored cities composed of children's building blocks. "This is more lyrical. I am trying to transmit love and tenderness and serenity through simplicity of form." In a third style, "social realism," he had documented a phase of Brasília's history that had already passed, when the houses in the North Wing of the Plano were still all wooden, gawdy little hotels for lovemaking, mostly, with names like Bagdad, Xango, Dinos, and Londres. His studies of them reminded me of Hopper, without the bleakness. But Milton Ribeiro had not seen the work of Edward Hopper.

Though Brasília's social structure is still evolving, one part asserted itself early on: the rich-poor cleavage along color lines. This was really part of the national structure, a pre-existing mold that was too strong for the new city to break out of. The government had expropriated the District at one dollar per acre and in the beginning was selling it at thirty cents per square foot. Many people bought lots sight unseen, as an investment. Even a few Americans, like Roy Rogers and Mary Martin, joined the land rush. Almost anyone could afford an apartment in the *superquadras,* and in the beginning ministers and chauffeurs were neighbors, on equal footing. But gradually a number of factors conspired to drive the poor out of the Plano. First, inflation: as monthly payments were "indexed" to keep apace with the rabid inflation of the post-Juscelino period, they became increasingly difficult to make for a low-income *pedreiro* (mason) or *motorista,* whose wage was not rising commensurately. The arrival of capitalism, as the construction and sale of space in the *superquadras* was turned over to private enterprise, drove up the prices of the apartments further. This did not affect the situation of the poor who already owned apartments, but it acted as an inducement for them to sell. At the same time they had already been getting the feeling that this was not their *ambiente,* anyway. Most of them had never dwelt in an apartment. Not knowing how to use the space, they partitioned off the big room and invited relatives to move in, which increased the friction with their white-collar neighbors, from whom they had already been getting the cold shoulder. By selling their apartments, they could make a killing, buy a car, a television, and everything they'd always wanted, and move into a simple *barraca* in Taguatinga, which was more agreeable in any case. And in a few years, when real estate in Taguatinga went out of sight, they could sell again at a great profit and move to a *barraca* in Ceilândia. It was not so much discrimination that expelled the poor from the Plano, as economics, and to a certain extent, they themselves rejected Niemeyer's utopia.

In Brazil, the poor generally mean the nonwhite, but to suggest that the country has racial problems, that there is active discrimination on the basis of pigmentation, is something that no one wishes to hear, especially from an American. The majority of Brazilians pay little mind to skin color, except to compliment each other's rich tones. There are at least thirty separate words used to make subtle distinctions among racial hybrids, and they are always spoken with an undercurrent of endearment, and never with the sort of hostility that goes with the ethnic slurs in the American vocabulary. Ana, for example, who had several friends called Ana Maria, usually referred to the one who was black as Ana Maria Prêtinha, "(dear) little black Ana Maria." As a child in Floriano she attended soccer games in which a player who missed an easy shot was compared by the crowd to a garbage-picking vulture if he was black, and to an immature cockroach if white, and no one took offense. According to her birth certificate, Ana is *morena,* or dark-skinned. The difference between *morena* and *prêto* in Brazil is not as charged with status as the difference between "brown" and "black" in Jamaica, though *morenos,* who already have white blood, have less trouble mixing with whites. "It is common for an upward-mobile individual, especially a male, to take a spouse several shades lighter," anthropologist Charles Wagley wrote in one of his many good books about Brazil. But "unions between very dark and very light people are considered undesirable and cause embarrassment to the individuals." My own experience confirms the accuracy of this. Our marriage raised no eyebrows in Brazil. As far as the Leonias family was concerned, Ana had married well, as Tété had by wedding Marco Aurelio, who was also white. I even sensed from the family a slightly deferential attitude toward Marco and me which I can only explain by the fact that we were white. On the other hand, marriage with a *prêto legítimo* would not have been deemed good; blacks were all right to be friends with, even close friends, but not to marry, and for a *branco* to marry a *prêto* would have been most peculiar. Brazilian racism is a subtle and touchy thing. I only ran into one blatant case of it in Brasília, from a member of the board of directors of the Yacht Club, who confided to me with palpable pride, "I'm really not supposed to say this, because it's against the constitution, but we have no black members." The increasing number of newspaper stories about discrimination and occasionally the lyrics of a song, like those of a 1976 hit, "Would you have the same love for Jesus if he had been a black man?" would indicate that there is a growing consciousness of racism in the country; but most Brazilians are still adamant that it does not exist. The important point is that it is more ingenuous than the overt, aggressive American brand—no burning crosses are planted on people's lawns in Brazil—and that a supportiveness, a sense of shared humanity, runs through the society at every level, transcending invidious color distinctions. "The Brazilian racism is paternalistic," a white man told me. "You don't do it out of hate but to be protective, because these people are inferiors." I asked what he meant by inferior. "Not in terms of native intelligence, but culturally and economically," he said. A few decades ago sociologist Oraci Noguiera distinguished between the American "race prejudice of origin," in which all people of known black ancestry, regardless of physical appearance, are discriminated against, and the Brazilian "race prejudice of mark," where physical traits like dark skin, thick lips, and kinky hair are what give rise to discrimination. But this is not entirely satisfactory. I spoke with David Vidal, the New York *Times'* Rio correspondent in 1978, who had written a controversial article called "Many Blacks Shut Out of Brazil's 'Racial Paradise.'" "Movement in things like race are glacial, because the problem is so pervasive," Vidal, himself a *moreno* Puerto Rican, said. "In Brazil people will give you the names of black athletes and entertainers as proof that they have no racism. They will not for the life of them acknowledge the very condemnatory circumstantial evidence that it does exist. In America the problem has been defined, and the group has benefited from it. I would say the difference is that Brazilian racism is worse for the group and better for the individual and in the United States it is worse for the individual and better for the group. And Brazilian racism is tempered by the fact that miscegenation is accepted, while in America it is not." A puzzling aspect of my wife's move to America was her change in status from *morena* to black. "I only learned that there was discrimination when I got to America," she said. Her reaction was, I think, typically Brazilian. "Racism is something that exists largely in people's minds. If you think it exists, it exists. If you don't, it doesn't occur to you."

By 1964, the poor in Brasília had withdrawn to the satellite cities, leaving the Plano to the still rather amorphous *classe media,* which is predominantly white but includes those blacks and *morenos* with sufficient *poder aquisitivo,* or "acquisitive capacity." I first heard the term *poder aquisitivo* on the lips of a real estate agent. It is useful in distinguishing the ambitious from the majority of Brazilians, for whom the concept of "getting ahead" is alien, who are grounded in often miserable circumstances by their deep humility, fatalism, and almost a kind of fear. The barriers that exist between the satellite cities and the Plano, for example, are largely psychological on the part of those without *poder aquisitivo.* Ana remembers how Iraci was criticized by her relatives: "How can you let your daughter buy a car? How can you let her take courses in the Plano? You don't have the means." In spite of their apprehension, Ana found that the opportunities of the Plano were within easy grasp. Many of her childhood friends in the satellite cities are now career girls inhabiting *superquadras,* which is probably where she would be if we hadn't met.

The quality of life in the *superquadra* is a topic of fierce debate. On one hand are the partisans. The ideal was perhaps best put forth by Juscelino: "Brasília is a unique city in Brazil, and perhaps in the world, in that it does not divorce itself from nature. Lúcio Costa and Oscar Niemeyer, in their conception of what the future capital should be like, believed above all in the necessity of creating a work that would be an extension of the *cerrado.* Thus, the city and the landscape which served as its base, would interpenetrate, commingle, merge. In all the great urban centers, as the values of civilization spread, the distance is accentuated between what man has created and the nature that encompasses. But in Brasília, the phenomenon was inverted." Compare the impression of Selden Rodman, an American deeply sympathetic to many aspects of Brazil, in 1977: "Here, in rectangular *supercuadros [sic]* of glass so soul-shrinking in scale and impersonal that even the bureaucrats who are obliged to live in them develop paranoid traits, no casual intercourse or creative impulses are possible. Accessible only by private automobile, no walkways are provided for pedestrians; food must be imported; communication is by electronics; and the living quarters of those who provide the labor and services are relegated to rings of satellite communities so distant that visitors are unaware that the majority of the capital's inhabitants live in them." Or that of veteran foreign correspondent Tad Szulc two years earlier: "My own feeling is that Brasília, in its way, is the coldest, most impersonal—even dehumanized—city that I have ever seen. It is so insanely functional that one wonders whether it was built for people or for automatons. Residents of the Plano Piloto live in identical '*superquadra*' complexes. . . . Each building has about two hundred families. . . . This works out to twenty-two hundred families (ten thousand human beings) in each wholly integrated and virtually self-sufficient *superquadra* concrete village . . . curiously . . . Niemeyer . . . failed to equip the *superquadra* apartments with balconies, as if to avoid any external signs of life in his buildings." Horror of Brasília is not confined to foreigners. Even Ana's Uncle Francisco, having transferred his *querência,* his pride of place, from Floriano to Rio, "wouldn't live there for a million dollars. When I see these white buildings all the same, the same height and everything, it reminds me of a cemetery. All the employees of the Bank of Brazil there live in the same *superquadras,* work at the same place, and on the weekend, go to the Bank of Brazil Club, where they sit around and talk about the same thing: what happened at work. You've already worked all week long. Why talk about it on your days off?"

Physically, life in the *superquadra* is like being on a campus. The landscaping is lush and attractive, though few *cerrado* trees are left. The Corbusian indepndent towers, separated by green spaces, are often criticized for their coldness and impersonality, but the Brazilians have had no trouble relating to them, or infusing them with *calor humano.* Were Brasília at the latitude of Boston, it would probably be grim indeed, with an appalling suicide rate; but at the very geographic heart of South America, it seems to me to be one of the world's most healthy and amiable urban complexes. In 1977 there were only ninety suicide attempts, thirty-four of which worked. In the same year five hundred and ninety-seven were admitted for psychiatric treatment. Both figures represented a substantial decrease from previous years.

In part Costa's thoughtful touches must be credited for the contentment in the *superquadras*. With no *bloco* over six stories (Niemeyer wanted them higher), they avoid the depressing stacked-up feeling of other instant cities such as the Bronx's Co-Op City. And the *pilotis* were a stroke of genius. In residential Brasília, the ascent of each superstructure is delayed for a floor, and the *blocos* stand on pillars, like dolmens. The space beneath them serves as shelter from the sudden rains that lash down without warning, as a common meeting ground for residents of the building, a place for potted trees, a trysting spot for teenage lovers. But the character of the Brazilian people must also be recognized. There is none of that Anglo-Saxon reserve in the elevators, none of that staring at the ceiling and not daring to address, even visually, the other passengers. In the *superquadras*, before the elevator doors have even closed, the passengers have usually struck up a conversation, and by the time they reach their floor, everyone is friendly.

The occupants of Bloco H, Superquadra 312 North, are mostly young couples with growing families. The doors are not locked and children are constantly wandering in and out of apartments and playing in the hallway. The mothers have companionship and babysit for each other, and in the evening families on the same hall frequently get together for a *seresta*, a songfest with everyone sitting on the floor and passing the guitar. The exterior of the building, when we were last there, was blackening with a fungus that assaults untreated concrete in the tropics. The occupants had asked the owner of the *bloco* to do something about it, but crying poverty, he had refused, and so they had taken up a collection and were getting the building painted themselves.

The *superquadras* are as disparate as the housing in any good-sized city. Some *blocos* have already degenerated, in less than two decades, into near slums. In other words, a doorman won't let you into the building with short pants. One often sees banners of professional soccer teams draped from the windows. In each *superquadra* there is a school. The schools' reputations vary considerably, and parents in the Plano are as concerned about getting their children into the good ones as parents in American suburbs are with moving into the right school district. Each *superquadra* also has its own place of worship. Most are Catholic. A few are Protestant churches or synagogues. At 315 South there is a Buddhist temple, serving one hundred and eighty Japanese families who are scattered over the District. I visited it with Dr. Dinant da Silva Ramalho Cruz, an ebullient city planner for the District who spent several mornings showing me the city. We were received by the padre, as Dr. Dinant called him, a venerable man in black robes. Dr. Dinant knelt at the altar before a gilded statue of the Bodhisattva. "This Buddha is so *thin,*" he exclaimed. "This one I can believe in. But *aquêle Buddha barriguda*—that fat Buddha—I can't believe he has spirituality. Where can I buy one?" he asked the padre, who didn't seem offended, and said he might be able to order one from São Paulo.

"One-eleven South, 202 North, and 309 South are inhabited by congressmen, 408 through 414 South are low-income *superquadras* for the poor, 112 and 113 South are for military bigwigs." I was driving around, on another occasion, with a bright young protégé of Dr. Dinant named Marcio Vilas-Boas. "The *interquadras* have separate identities, too. Some cater to women, with boutiques selling stockings and handbags; some specialize in used cars; 109 South is a meeting place for Bohemians and gays. The ones near the Hospital Sector have an inordinate number of drugstores. But every *interquadra* has, at the very least, a bakery and a drugstore. It is really like, if you can visualize it, an American shopping mall, with a street running through instead of a pedestrian walkway." Vilas-Boas,

Alex Shoumatoff

who was in his mid-thirties, was obsessed with ventilation in the same way that many young architects and urbanists in the temperate zones are obsessed with the problems of heating. For his masters degree, which he had gotten from Rice, he had written a thesis called "Wind-Tunnel Simulation of Wind-Flow Around Buildings and Within Urban Areas." Now he was putting the finishing touches on his doctoral thesis, which was about the climatic adaptation of vernacular and primitive houses in America, Brazil, Israel, and Africa. "The trouble with the Corbusian glass box," he said, "is that it is poorly adapted to the tropics. When glass is exposed all day to the sun, there is tremendous solar heat gain. I went into the Palace of Agriculture at eleven o'clock the other morning and even though it was air conditioned, I *had to take my coat off* because of the solar heat gain. Glass lets through short-wavelength radiation, you see, which is converted into heat. The heat in turn generates long-wavelength radiation, to which glass is impervious. If you are in an air-conditioned room that is exposed to radiation, the temperature of the thermostat will have to be much lower to keep the room at the same temperature as it is outside in the shade, no? That is because of solar heat gain." He gestured passionately at a ministry whose glass exterior was encrusted with air conditioners. "This city has one of the best climates in the world—and look at all those air conditioners. Air conditioning is not only a waste of energy, but it is also totally inappropriate to dehydrate a climate that is already more than dry enough."

"What's the solution, then?" I asked. "Screens?"

"No. Screens block too much air. You'd have to enlarge your windows to an extent that would be undesirable for security reasons. *Brise-soleils* help."

The *brise-soleil* is a stationary fixture, usually a concrete slab or a metal sheet, which is aligned vertically along a window to shield it from direct sunlight. Marcio's favorite *brise-soleils* in Brasília were on the new, cylindrical Central Bank Building—

176

fixed concrete blades which had been ingeniously staggered after careful study of the sun's trajectory. The Central Bank Building is the Fort Knox of Brazil, with the nation's reserves, billions in gold bullion and diamonds, kept stashed on six subterranean floors.

As far as Marcio was concerned, the climatic adaptation of all the ministries and most of the buildings in the Southern Commercial Sector was *péssima*—wretched. In the beginning, when the ministries were first occupied, some of the ministers had two offices. When the sun was at full strength they simply moved to the other side of the building. Later, Venetian blinds were installed, and the windows were opened. But the trouble with blinds and open windows is that in a good south wind rain falling in the Monumental Sector has been known to enter the windows of the ministries horizontally and thoroughly drench the functionaries within. At Christmastime the secretaries in some ministries open or shut the blinds on different floors in such a way that a huge Christmas tree is traced on the side of the building. Other ministries are experimenting with reflective glass to cut down radiation. The drawback with reflective glass is that while you can see out during the day, night brings the reverse effect. Marcio said he hadn't solved the ventilation question yet, but he took me to his house, where, by a cunning system of removable glass panels and fixed blinds, he had achieved maximum cross-ventilation without compromising the safety of his family. "Watch how when I open the front door, the mobile in the kitchen starts turning," he said with the exaggerated seriousness of someone who did not want to seem proud.

———

One of Ana's dear friends in the Plano was a nurse whom I shall call Artemisia, though she had in fact an equally lovely classical name. Artemisia lived in an unpretentious *superquadra* and was going through an ugly divorce. When she had discovered that her husband was cheating on her, she had had the effrontery to begin seeing other men. The moral code in Brazil is so prejudiced against women that her husband was trying to use her "whorelike" behavior to gain custody of their two children and the apartment, which they had gotten through her job. Artemisia had lost the first round in court, and unless she won the appeal, she expected to lose her children on the grounds of her moral unfitness to be their mother and to be thrown into the street. Brasília has the highest rate of marital failure in the country. One Sunday afternoon, when we were over at Artemisia's, we started talking about it.

"You know Dr. Alan, the lawyer?" asked a friend of Artemisia's named Filomena. "He's separating eight or ten a day." Artemisia and Filomena, who was separated herself, had met at a club for *desquitados,* as legally separated people are called, which had been tremendously popular until the police had closed it down a few months before. I asked why. "Because it was becoming a pickup place," Filomena said. She was leafing through an article entitled "Sex During Carnaval . . . Is It Better?" in a *Cosmopolitan* imitation called *Nova.*

Artemisia blamed the high separation rate (actual divorces, which were only legalized in 1977, are costly and still quite rare) on the dullness of Brasília and the relatively emancipated condition of its female population. "The *carioca* goes to the beach," she said, "but here, imprisoned in the *superquadras,* what is there to do? Work and TV. That is your life here. My husband spent his weekends in a half-stupor, watching the soccer games. We never went anywhere. We had no communication, and women like to communicate, you know. A lot of the problem has to do with lack of comprehension on the part of the male. The women here work, though the men would prefer they stayed home and minded the house. The men won't help clean the floor because it's a humiliation. But the women are free and as their frustration deepens, the couple grows further apart, until finally they end up separating."

Other explanations were put forward: Ana mentioned Brasília's extreme youth and lack of structure; the way young people who were lonely and far from their families in a brand-new city that lacked the rigid social structures in which they had been brought up often met at work and married hardly knowing each other.

Filomena suggested that couples in Brasília were too much on top of each other. It is the only city in Brazil where everyone goes home for lunch. The lunch hour is actually two hours long, and for federal and District employees, bus service is provided. One would think this would help keep families together, but somehow it seems to work the other way.

I was interested in the connection between television and marital breakdown. Television is an immensely important part of present-day Brazilian life. Of the three heralds of progress, the three machines after whose arrival life can never be the same (the automobile and the telephone being the other two), the television has achieved by far the deepest penetration. Wherever there is electricity, the television follows. Sets are available on easy terms, and even the most humble shacks are lit up nightly with its ghostly glow. Before a poor man will buy a refrigerator, he will buy a television, and because there is so much illiteracy and unemployment, so much isolation and hunger for knowledge of the world beyond, the television in Brazil has an almost frightening power. In the backlands, the impact of television exceeds that of roads. The number of people who are hooked on it, who spend the majority of their waking hours in front of it, must number in the scores of millions. I could get no precise figures and no answers about programming philosophy or the possible effect television might be having, because no one in Brasília who was in the industry was willing to see me. Some believe that there is a close and perhaps conspiratorial relationship between television and the government. "I think the government is making television available to everyone to keep people from getting together and transmitting ideas," said a leftist critic of the regime. "You notice how whenever there's a strike, three soccer games are run back to back. And you know the Brazilians: you can't talk to them when there's a soccer game on the television. But I think the strategy is going to backfire. When the people see that there is an Iran that reacts, that says 'enough,' or that movie *The Seven Samurai,* with its beautiful political message, is shown, they will start thinking. The government is so dumb that it doesn't even censor with intelligence." (This, too, was a pre-*abertura* conversation.)

I met many with misgivings about television. Some were worried about Brazil becoming a nation of zombies. Some complained of the emphasis of the evening news on violence instead of social problems. Others were concerned about the effect of sudden exposure of global carnage and chicanery to the innocent people of the backlands: what would they make of Soviet-American missile buildup, terrorism in Northern Ireland, or strikes in England, which were run by them without analysis or explanation? Still others, having discerned the well-known corrupting-of-the-youth effect, complained of the miniskirts that were being worn on television and how their children were being led to think that smoking was a "cool" thing to do. I am personally disquieted by the introduction of gratuitous, pathological American violence into Brazilian culture through such popular dubbed shows as "Baretta" and "Kojak" (there is already plenty of violence in Brazil, but it is of a more straightforward and comprehensible nature, with poverty and jealousy the main motives), and the way neighborhoods seem to break down shortly after television reaches them.

I could see this beginning to happen in Sobradinho, though it was still a friendlier place than anywhere I knew in the United

States. Nowhere did I watch so much television as I did in Sobradinho. There was a set in every home I visited. The set was left on almost constantly. Conversation competed with it; one eye was always cast in its direction. The same was true in the Plano. At the same time she was criticizing television, Artemisia had two sets going, a small black-and-white in her bedroom, and a big color in the livingroom.

The most stultifying part of the fare are of course the commercials, which are shown over and over, the same one, in the course of a program. And when there is a shortage of new material the same shows are repeated from one night to the next. Yet between commercials there is much of interest. I enjoyed the old movies, starring people like Jerry Lewis, Danny Kaye, and Abbott and Costello; the reruns of "Bonanza" took me back twenty years to childhood and undoubtedly contributed to the nostalgic effect that Sobradinho was having on me. Old Hollywood Westerns, called *bangy-bangys,* were often aired. One of the most popular cowboy stars is a lusty actor named Rex Allen, who wore a tall Stetson to disguise his shortness. Allen became only moderately famous in America in the forties, but three decades later has acquired a second, far more substantial following in South America. Of the indigenous programs "Planet of the Men" was perhaps my favorite, with outrageous satirical skits like "Laugh-In" or "Saturday Night Live"; the Brazilians' capacity to laugh at themselves is highly developed. There are interminable talent and quiz shows in which Everyman tries to amass instant fame or fortune. In 1977 a whiz-kid from a *favela* in Rio answered a succession of impossible questions correctly, winning a beautiful house and a car for his mother, and because there was an almost hysterical identification with his rags-to-riches success, he became an instant national hero. But the most important events on television are the *novelas.* I resisted becoming involved in them because they would have robbed me of my evenings. The *novelas* are prime-time soap operas which have obsessed the Brazilian public to a degree that American television has only achieved with "Roots," "Holocaust," and briefly the "Mary Hartman, Mary Hartman" series. They are a kind of popular theater with a following of millions, and often the best of the country's professionals, writers like Jorge Amado and actresses like Sonia Braga, become involved in their production. While delivering sufficient melodrama to be appealing to the lowest common denominator, they are often, because they mirror the society so truthfully, indirectly or subliminally instructive. I remember once entering a house in which a violent argument seemed to be in progress. "You're not my father!" a girl was screaming. "Anyone who abandons his family as you did doesn't deserve the name of father." The girl, I realized when I reached the livingroom, was in the television, the heroine of a *novela*. In 1979 the hit *novela* was "Aritana," about a semiacculturated Indian who was struggling to keep his people's lands in the Amazon from being ripped off by a developer with whose niece he had fallen in love. The girl fell in love with him, too, but only after she had duplicitously collaborated with her uncle in a scheme to make Aritana sign a piece of paper that would forfeit all his tribe's property. Almost everybody in Brasília followed "Aritana," and much of the conversation was about how they thought he would fare in the coming evening's installment. Watching television in Brasília is by far and away the dominant, and for many the exclusive, leisure activity. There is a joke about dinner at the home of a couple who are glued to their set: during the first commercial the wife turns on the oven, during the second she sets the table, during the third she says grace. In the *superquadras* the only windows that are not lit with its glow in the evening are black, because the people there are not home.

Toward the end of the afternoon Artemisia's seventeen-year-old daughter burst into the flat with her fiancé and half a dozen of the bushiest potted ferns I'd ever seen. *Samambaias,* as ferns are delightfully called, had been on sale at the plant shop in the *interquadra*. *"Puxe,"* her twelve-year-old sister said, "this place is going to be a forest." A rage for houseplants had lately been sweeping through the *superquadras*. Some apartments were veritable jungles. "A desperate care is given to houseplants here," Dr. Dinant had said. "Maybe because the people feel the lack of a house with terrain to plant. Maybe because they just need things to do. Brazilians love music and plants. You can tell from the suaveness of our speech. My neighbor plays the piano. I have to listen to her. All day long."

I took a picture of Artemisia's oldest daughter posing wantonly among the ferns in her short shorts. A week later we heard that the girl had been killed in a car accident. She and her fiancé had been returning from a camping trip, he at the wheel, she beside him, when the car collided with a truck with such force that her eyes were apparently knocked out of her head. We called on Artemisia a few days after the funeral; I had made a blow-up of her daughter's picture, the last taken of her. Artemisia seemed to be recovering, but the color was still gone from her face, the irreverent wit that was so important a part of her strength had been silenced. She told us she was feeling better since she had been to a medium and spoken with her daughter's ghost. Her daughter had told her that she was happy, having been reunited with her grandmother, who had died several months earlier. She asked Artemisia to forgive her father and said that she (who had often sided with her father in his quarrels with Artemisia) was suffering for the way she had treated her mother; and asked Artemisia to pray for her.

It is common for Brazilians, even those who are not active practitioners of *macumba* or *espiritismo,* to turn to the mediums in times of distress. The difference between *macumba* and *espiritismo* is that the former frequently involves black magic, while the latter is a predominantly white-magic cult and has more ties with Christianity. Many prominent and educated Brazilians are

183

adherents of *espiritismo*. Like Pepe, the manager of the Hotel Nacional. One Sunday afternoon, at Manuel Mendes' country *granja,* Pepe took a foot of Manuel's wife, who is paralyzed from the waist down, and blew on it, and then, still holding it, started to cry; and as the pain passed from her foot into his being, his eyes grew large. On another occasion we visited a woman in Sobradinho who had been left by her husband years before, and unable to find a man, had taken to drink. *Pinga* had gotten the better of her, and she was sitting with a group of friends and talking about her problem. The other night, when she had been drunk, she claimed that someone had entered the house, pushed her against the wall, and hit her repeatedly on the head. But her children had said that was impossible because they had heard nothing and there were no signs of a break-in. At night, she said, she rolled back and forth, pitching in her bed breaking out alternatively into hot and cold sweats. One of her friends suggested that she had been possessed by the spirit of a woman who, having been left by her husband, roamed the streets drinking and smoking and preventing similarly rejected women from getting together with members of the other sex. "You should have the spirit driven out by a *macumbeira,*" the friend said.

Once when they were living in Gama, Terezinha, Waldemar's wife, went to a *macumbeira* to see if the woman could cure him of his drinking problem. Terezinha had heard about the priestess from a friend for whom the woman had performed an abortion. The *macumbeira* agreed to do some *trabalho,* some "work," for Waldemar, and in the next weeks she came often to Terezinha, demanding payment. "The spirit wants a skirt of such-and-such a color; the spirit wants a hundred cruzeiros," she would say, explaining that unless she was given these things, she couldn't perform the service. Terezinha complied, but there was no noticeable change in Waldemar's condition. At last Terezinha refused to give her further payment, and the *macumbeira* said, "I

184

will put such a spell on you, that on Saturday you will step in front of a car and be killed." Terrified, Terezinha waited for Saturday to come, but on the day before she was supposed to meet her end, word swept through the street that the *macumbeira* and her twelve-year-old daughter had been found dead in the cemetery, buried to their necks and with a goat's foot placed beside them. In time it was learned that her *compadre,* a man who was also versed in voodoo, had done the killings. The priestess had gone to him and explained that she had such a backlog of *macumba* to do, for which she had already been paid, that she feared she would never get it done. The *compadre* said he would do it for her, but in exchange for her daughter, to whom he had always been attracted. Reluctantly, she agreed, but when the *compadre* came to her and said the work had been done, she had refused to let him have her daughter, and in his rage the man had killed them both, taken their bodies to the cemetery, and buried them in a ritual fashion.

The automobile has undoubtedly opened new dimensions of mobility for those Brazilians who can afford one, but at the same time there is scarcely a family to whom it has not brought grief. Accidents with cars are the principal cause of unnatural death, and Brasília has the greatest density of car owners (one car for every 8.3 people as opposed to one for every 18.6 people in the whole of Brazil) as well as the highest accident rate (in 1972 .64 collisions were reported for every thousand inhabitants, as opposed to .58 in Rio and São Paulo, and five hundred pedestrians were reported struck. Both figures are deceptive, however, as the vast majority of accidents go unreported.). I myself have narrowly escaped being run down in Brasília three

bumper sticker that said THIS CAR RUNS ON ALCOHOL (IN THE MOTORIST).

But the main reason for the accidents in Brasília, and in the country at large, is the attitude of the drivers. The Brazilian motorist drives with gusto and abandon, like a child with his first toy, and when he sees pedestrians in his path, he speeds up rather than slows down, scattering them like chickens. As in other countries where people drive maniacally, Darwinian selection of the physically fittest is still operative on the human population. "How humbly that man crossed the road," Ana observed once as we were cruising down the North Wing, "as if he were guilty of something terrible."

"Yes," I said. "He looked like he was running for his life."

A specialist in the District's highway system, who had previously helped design the national system, put the matter in perspective for me. "For most Brazilians, motoring is still a new and strange experience," he said. "Only 4.7 percent of our roads are even paved; compare this with 95 percent in West Germany, 80.8 percent in the United States, 13.6 percent in Argentina, and 7.4 percent in India. Those who are killed on the roads are victims of the accelerated acquisition of progress, of all that happened in five years instead of fifty. Having just reached the motorized condition, the Brazilian driver is now on his honeymoon with the car. He has not been educated about its dangers. A tremendous effort is needed." Soon after this conversation a shocking short, showing the mangled car of someone who had tried to pass to the right, started to appear on the television in the spots reserved for commercials.

Several weeks before our last visit, the Leonias family was dealt a terrible blow, when Dona Joana's distinguished-looking brother, João Nepomuceno de Jesus, was killed by a car in the State of São Paulo. Uncle Joe was the man who said *"Vai embora, meninos,"* shooing us from the wedding party. He had always had a patriarchal idea of the family and after its exodus from Floriano, he had wanted everyone to be reunited in the same place. But it hadn't worked out that way. He himself had sold his floating restaurant, with its fish-shaped menus, and moved to the city of Parnaíba, on the coast of Piauí, where for a time he had an elegant shoestore. But then Daniel, the oldest of his sister's children, persuaded him to come to the city of Rezende in São Paulo, and at the time of his death he was working there as the comptroller in a British-owned factory of farm machinery. Having come home from work, he had decided at the last minute to go out and buy a chicken, and he was crossing the road when the car came whizzing around the corner, got him behind the legs and threw him up into the air. As he came down his head went through the windshield. Bleeding profusely from his nose and mercifully in a coma, with both legs snapped above the knee, he was first taken to the hospital at Rezende and later transferred to intensive care at Volta Redonda, where he died at five o'clock the following afternoon. Because the man at the wheel was a godfather of one of Daniel's children, the family did not prosecute him. For a year no one in the de Jesus family could dance at Carnaval; to be seen letting themselves go in public would have been an impropriety.

Uncle Joe was killed about four miles from the place where, a little more than two years earlier, there was another fatal car accident, whose repercussions were felt throughout the country. The vehicles involved were an Opel sedan and a tractor-trailer. The victim was Juscelino Kubitschek, hurrying to Rio on the rain-slicked highway.

Juscelino's funeral in the glass cathedral drew about three million mourners, the largest crowd that had ever assembled in the capital. Among the many eulogies and reminiscences of him which continue to appear with great frequency in the nation's printed media was one in the *Correio Brasiliense*. "As a doctor," it said, "he cured the great collective disease of the Brazilian nation—the inferiority complex." He had been buried a week when I first arrived in Brasília, so from the beginning I was conscious of him. Though he was the only one of the "Three Musketeers" of Brasília I didn't meet, I felt I knew him through his writing, in which his personal warmth and simplicity are plainly evident, and through interviews with his numerous friends, whom I sought out at every opportunity. Juscelino embodied the best of what is great about the Brazilian people, the fundamental goodness which is the nation's most precious asset; he seemed the soul of goodness.

"He was beautiful, *muito alegre, admirável, extraordinário,* most human—someone you were accustomed to meet only in legends, like the *Thousand and One Nights,*" said Colonel Lelio Graça, his private secretary for years. They had known each other since Diamantina, when Lelio was twenty and a soldier stationed there, and Juscelino seventeen. Later, at the hospital in Belo Horizonte, they met again. Lelio, now thirty, was a secretary at the hospital, and Juscelino a medical captain. Juscelino became the mayor, and Lelio joined the state police, retiring in 1947 with the rank of colonel. In 1959 he came to Brasília as a newspaperman, and after a year joined NOVACAP as a translator of English and French. "I learned those languages almost all by myself," he said. "To tell the truth, I learned English by teaching others. I only studied it formally for three months. As I was very poor, in the fourth I could not pay. My wife Paquita was one of my French pupils." Later in 1960 he became Juscelino's private secretary in the Dawn Palace. "I still am his secretary, without remuneration," he said. "I even buy the stamps myself. My recompense has been the sincere friendship of a worthy and admirable man." He still wrote in Juscelino's name when an extraordinary humanitarian effort was indicated. Most recently, it had worked to get a family out of Rumania so they could join their father, who had defected to Brazil. Lelio last saw Juscelino in 1974, when he came to their golden wedding anniversary. Lelio showed me a photograph of Juscelino hugging him and Paquita in the cathedral, and a letter that Juscelino had written him from Paris, thanking Lelio for his "extreme loyalty" and "incomparable collaboration." A large oil painting of O Presidente hung in his study.

According to his calling card, Lelio was an "interpreter and translator from English and into English. Technology, Science, and Poetry." On his cluttered desk was a half-translated "psycho-pedagogical work" entitled "Locus of Control and Generosity in Learning Disabled, Normal Achieving, and Gifted Children." Next to it a book called *Russian in Record Time*. On his shelves eight editions of the Bible, including ones in French and Latin. "I am big on the Bible," he said. "My motto is 'childhood, love, and humility,' after St. Francis of Assisi. I don't believe in revolution. The terrorist is my brother. Niemeyer—his spirit is very elevated—but I don't understand why he is a communist. Maybe he didn't have a mother who educated him. Or maybe he couldn't stand this *porcaria* of a society."

Lelio and Paquita lived in 108 South, an older *superquadra* inhabited by people who were comfortably retired, mostly from government service. The apartment had an Old World flavor, except for the bathroom, which except for the bidet was pure American and had the only bathtub and closed shower stall in the District. "My wife is very creative," Lelio said. "She copied our bathroom from a motel where we spent the night in Florida." Even at eighty-one, Lelio's own energy seemed one step ahead of him. "I'm a licensed pilot. I'm crazy about the guitar. My photographic archives would take a month to go through. Have you read anything about the education of the mind?" he said, pulling down his volumes of Tolstoy's didactic works. One of his daughters was named Yasnaya. But mostly he was a poet. He recited his Portuguese version of an Edna St. Vincent Millay poem about Lidice.

It was deeply moving, and he was only able to get through two stanzas before he started to cry. "Paquita hates it when I read my poems," he blubbered, "because I can never get through them." Most of his verse was collected in an unpublished volume, "Brasília, Transamazonica, and Other Poems," and was about the capital and the new life it had brought to the country.

On weekends Lelio and his family would go to their *chácara*, on Kilometer 13 of the Brasília-Belo Horizonte Highway. There are two recreational options for the people in the Plano: either they frequent one of the twenty athletic clubs, which are also social clubs, along Lake Paranoá, or they have a place in the country. The people in the satellite cities for the most part have no recreational options. They suffer unknowingly from what is sometimes called recreation deprivation. The country places are based on the Texas ranch, and their most important feature is a large outdoor barbecue pit. There are several kinds of country place. The *latifúndio*, an estate with several thousand acres— almost a small fiefdom—is extinct in Brasília. The *fazenda* is generally a large ranch with cattle. Fazenda Torto, the president's country retreat—his Camp David—is only five minutes from the end of the North Wing. A *granja* is quite grand, too, but specializes in poultry. The emphasis of a *sítio* is agricultural, silvicultural, or horticultural—on plants, in other words. A *chácara* can be either a small farm or a weekend retreat. A *roça* is a subsistence garden, often with a modest dwelling for the people who are living from it. Sometimes the terms are used interchangeably: a poor man might boast of his *fazenda* when it is actually a *roça*, while it is fashionable among those who are sufficiently sure of themselves that they don't have to impress anybody to denigrate their *fazendas* and *granjas* by calling them *chácaras*. Lelio's country place was a good-sized *chácara*. It had about ten acres and a house with several bedrooms, plumbing, and a large, modern kitchen. There was even a small spiritist

191

chapel in which his daughter worshiped. Manuel Mendes' country place, eight miles farther down the Brasília-Belo Horizonte Highway, was more substantial. Large signs saying GRANJA BOA JARDIM guided the visitor to its entrance, and his weekend guests invariably included a foreign ambassador or two. Half a dozen hands lived at the *granja* full-time and looked after the turkeys and the crops. There were horses to ride, hammocks to rock in, boats to row on a small lake that had been created by damming the river. There was a pool and a telephone in the main house that said PISCINE, though only for effect, as the *granja* was over a mile from the nearest telephone pole. One room was devoted to gemstones, with which Manuel was willing to part for prices between those at Cristalina and those at the Hotel Nacional. We whiled away a few afternoons at Manuel's *granja* and one at Lelio's *chácara*. I had met Lelio and Paquita through their grandson, Rommel Castro, the chief of the Divulgation Section at DETUR, Brasília's Department of Tourism. As a teenager, he had become an accomplished sailor on Lake Paranoá, sailing a snipe, which is a sixteen-foot sloop with a cockpit. Lake Paranoá sailors have won three world championships in the snipe class. They often race in São Paulo and have even competed in Lake Forest, Illinois.

In Brazil February is the high point of the year, the month for which everyone has been waiting. The reason is that Carnaval, that four-day period of merrymaking, the original excuse for which has long been forgotten, usually comes in February. In 1979 it fell between the twenty-fourth and the twenty-seventh, though for many it actually began on the night of the twenty-third, a Friday, and since many danced till seven in the morning

of the twenty-eighth, which was Ash Wednesday and the start of
Lent, they spent the rest of the day sleeping it off, and didn't
report to work till the morning of the first. Many feel that
Carnaval is the most important institution in Brazil. As Almir
de Andrade has put it: "Carnaval is a protest—a gigantic
protest of delirious, lunatic multitudes against the formulas that
separate us from each other, against all the artifices that society
requires for its self-preservation." For the poor, many of whom
blow a whole year's savings on their Carnaval costume, it is
their one transcendent moment of release. Nothing in America—not Mardi Gras, not Woodstock—quite compares with its
letting go, its mass celebration of common humanity through
dance and charade.

In Brasília Carnaval is a relatively muted affair, "worse than
on the poorest back street of Rio," a *carioca* sniped. But
thousands of costumed revelers nevertheless flocked nightly to
the clubs along the lake, where blaring, many-piece bands with
names like Supersound 2000 played ceaselessly past dawn.
Some of the celebrants wore masks, some dressed as pirates or
sheiks, some had next to nothing at all. Groups of friends
arrived in matching outfits, and leopard-spotted leotards were
popular among the women. The theme of many costumes was
innocence: one girl who looked as if she wanted to get married
wore a wedding gown and others came as animals or Indians.
Everyone danced except those who stood on the sidelines
flinging coils of colored paper called *serpentinas* which embroiled
but did not seem to faze the dancers. It was impossible in the
bobbing sea of bodies not to be infected with the collective
euphoria, not to be transported to the universal plane of *alegria,*
not to let go, at least for the duration, of the jealously guarded
self.

DETUR had sponsored a competition for the best "block" of
revelers in the District. The prize money, fifteen thousand
cruzeiros, was not important. What mattered, most of the

contestants agreed, was winning the trophy and pleasing the crowd. Among the twelve entries was a group from Sobradinho that called itself the Black Ball. Ana's friend, Ana Maria Prêtinha, was one of the moving forces behind the Black Ball. Originally a *carioca,* she took her Carnaval seriously, and had been lovingly sewing her costume, which was almost entirely composed of feathers, for the past month. The *blocos* were to parade down W-3, a long service road in the South Wing which had been lined with bleachers and strung with illuminated globes in anticipation. A full division of revelers, like the ones who parade in Rio, is called an *Escola de Samba,* and many have thousands of members. It is led off by a woman called the *porta bandeira,* who carries the colors of the school. She wears eighteenth-century garb and a powdered wig, as does the *mestre sala,* an agile man who pirouettes around her, occasionally dropping to one knee and flourishing his fan. Each element in the procession is traditional and must be right. The *baianas,* large black women with bandanas and hooped skirts, must twirl with abandon and yet in unison. The hips of the scantily clad *sambistas* must rotate seductively while their legs jitterbug at breakneck speed. The *enrêdo,* the story that the group is trying to present, must be poignant. The *alegorias,* or floats, must be sumptuous, the *fantasias,* or costumes, dazzling. The *bateria,* or rhythm section, must lay down a steady, relentless beat. The rhythmic part of samba music, which is more important than the melodic part, is African in origin and little different from the drumming I have heard at *macumba* services and in the revivalist churches of rural Jamaica. All were perhaps inspired by the dense rhythmic field which insects and tree frogs produce at night in the equatorial forest. In a Carnaval procession several kinds of drums are often joined by *xeque-xeques,* tambourines, *cavaquinhos,* and an instrument called the *cuica* which makes a warped, rising sound like that of an undulating saw-blade. So critical is the *harmonia* between the rhythm section, dancing, and singing, that a frantic man runs around imploring everyone to keep together. But most important is perpetual sound and motion. If the judge catches one person who isn't dancing, or one who isn't singing, the whole group's chances are dashed.

A *bloco* is a miniature *Escola de Samba,* with only several hundred members. Some of the processional elements may be left out, but the spirit is undiminished. The *enrêdo* of the Black Ball was the dream of a child who finds himself in a fabulous garden, where he meets all his idols: Superman, Wonder Woman, Captain Marvel, Father Christmas, and a host of others, each of whom is represented by a member of the *bloco.* We took Ana Maria's mother, Dona Mercedes, to see her daughter; Rommel had given us tickets. There was a good crowd in the bleachers and lining the street, but nothing like the five hundred thousand for which DETUR had hoped. "In a few moments," the master of ceremonies announced over the speakers, "the asphalt of our street, W-3, which is as yet tranquil, will come to life with the *passarela* of the samba," and everybody cheered wildly. The Black Ball, who were fifth in the parade, went all out for the crowd, but it was the *candangos* of Nucleobandeirante who were judged the most animated, disciplined, and original *bloco,* and took the title.

Hardly had the citizens of the District recovered from Carnaval when feverish preparations for anther festivity began: the inauguration of the new president, João Batista Figueiredo. The "passing of the sash," as the ceremony was called, was scheduled for the morning of the fifteenth, and already a week beforehand ground crews consisting mostly of women in blue uniforms such as hospital patients wear, barefoot or wearing shower sandals, had begun sprucing up the Monumental Sector, repainting the lines on the roads and trimming excessively healthy sprouts of grass with their machetes. There was little to do, really, as the city was already immaculate. The most important thing was to see that every pole had a flag. The largest flag in the capital was in the Plaza of the Three Powers. It was roughly the size of a tennis court and flew from a heavy structure designed by Sérgio Bernardes, and was more like a tower than a pole and clashed with the ethereal lightness of Oscar's buildings. But perhaps it had been wise to err on the side of solidity, because the winds in the plaza were so violent that the flag, in shreds, had to be replaced once a month in a special military ceremony.

More important were the behind-the-scenes preparations having to do with the *abertura*. Figueiredo had been chosen by Geisel as his successor in part because he, too, wanted the country returned to democracy and the military relieved of its role as superintendent of the government. As a dictator, he would not be an entirely free agent because Geisel had already revoked the president's authority to remove congressmen and justices at will, and because he was answerable to an Army command whose views of how the country should be run were a good deal more conservative than those of Geisel or himself. Brazil was at an important turning point. Its precise situation would be described later that year by Norman Macrae, the deputy editor of *The Economist,* with the tart succinctness characteristic of that publication:

> The next few years, under a new president whose main passion is fortunately horseriding, will decide whether Brazil can move from a too interventionist military technocrat government (which is the fourth worst sort of government for a South American country to have) into becoming a Japanese-style near democracy with a more market-oriented economy (which is the best early hope for any development-ripe poor country in today's world).
> Or whether Brazil will be driven back into the vicious circle of the three worse and more usual sorts of South American governments, which are the military oppressive,

THE CAPITAL OF HOPE

the military populist, and the civilian populist—the last
two of which become so inflationary, corrupt, and Jacobin
that they spark coups by the military oppressives and start
the whole vicious circle again.

The situation was sensitive to larger, global conditions. Brazil
depended on Arab oil and foreign capital, and should the flow of
either, for some reason, stop, should one of the political and
economic thunderheads hovering over the international scene
suddenly burst, the return of democratic conditions to the
country would surely be set back. And then there were domestic
aggravations: Since the lifting of censorship and repression, the
Brazilian labor force, disgruntled and grossly underpaid, had
begun to exercise its new freedom of action and speech. By July
seven hundred and fifty thousand workers would have participated in forty-six strikes, causing the longest work stoppage
since 1953. And in the days immediately before the inauguration, the intransigence of MDB, the opposition party, was also
threatening the *abertura*. The man Geisel had entrusted with
laying the political groundwork for the opening was a crusty
professional named Petronio Portella. Portella had been governor of Piauí, then the president of Geisel's senate; and now he
would be Figueiredo's minister of justice, a close advisory
position. The current governor of Piauí was Portella's brother, a
doctor, and the mayor of Teresina, the capital of Piauí, was the
brother of Portella's secretary. "It's all in the family," a
congressman explained to me. Both officials were *bionicos,* a term
derived from the television program "The Bionic Woman," and
meaning appointed rather than elected, with the implication
that they were programmed automatons rather than possessors
of any political convictions of their own. Since the revolution all
governors and mayors and one third of the Senate had been
bionicos, and that was what the row with MDB, which stands for
the Brazilian Democratic Movement, was about. Several frac-

tious MDB senators had refused to serve on the Senate Administrative Committee because two other senators on the committee were bionic. It was a great impasse, the first time in history that MDB had not been represented on the Administrative Committee, and until it was resolved, the new Senate could not begin to function. But if anyone could smooth things over, it was Portella. "He has many friends in MDB and is hoping for things that for others would be impossible," said his secretary, an earthy blonde named Maria do Ampara, who wore, clipped to either earlobe, a sparkling aquamarine the size of a twenty-five-cent piece. I had caught her in a corridor of the Congress. Voices carried easily down the corridor, which was long and sealed, like an airport conduit, so she kept hers at a whisper. "He is *dialogando* with them now. What they are talking about I can't tell you. But MDB has to show some sense. The president has promised an *abertura,* but only with the cooperation of MDB. We don't want anarchy."*

But in spite of these problems, the general mood before the inauguration was distinctly positive. People felt as if they had at last put a bad time behind them, as if things were finally looking up; those who were at all aware of what was going on, that is. The majority of the population, whose lives were not affected by changes in Brasília in any way that they could see (and I would include most of the people in the satellite cities in this category), felt nothing one way or the other. They would watch the passing of the sash on the television, and when it was over, stay tuned, waiting for the *novelas* to begin. But the liberal intelligentsia seemed cheered. There was even a rumor that Niemeyer would attend the ceremony—his first official appearance in Brasília since the military had taken over. And though Figueiredo had not been elected by the people, an effort was being made to

---

*Early in 1980, Portella died of a sudden heart attack, but the progress toward democracy continues.

involve them in the festivities. Ten thousand of the country's most outstanding schoolchildren were being bused to the capital, where they would salute the new head of state with a special program of singing and dancing in the Emilio Médici Gymnasium of Sport; and the Independent Youth of Padre Miguel, who had won the coveted trophy for the smartest School of Samba in Rio a fortnight earlier, was also coming. Their triumphant procession down W-3, which we witnessed, would draw the largest crowd in Brasília since Juscelino's funeral: over a mile long and five people deep on either side of the street, with people sitting on the concrete awnings of the stores and threatening to bring them down—a frightening crush of people which dispersed as calmly and mysteriously as it had materialized.

A week before the American delegation was to arrive, the Secret Service came quietly to town and started making its preparations. I met one of them in the lobby of the Embassy. He was so suspiciously nondescript, with his elevator shoes, his dacron-polyester suit, and a slight bulge under the left armpit, that I immediately guessed his business. When I saw him at work a week later he had inserted a pink plastic radio receiver in one ear, to which he was listening attentively while scanning his field of vision for sudden movements, as a fisherman watches the surface of a pond for a rise. I asked if he wore a bulletproof vest. "What for?" he answered. "If somebody was doing a righteous effort, he wouldn't be using a .38." I asked how many Secret Service were in Brasília and he said that was classified. According to the *Correio Brasiliense,* the entire American delegation consisted of one hundred and ten people. Headed by Joan Mondale, the vice-president's wife, it included such assorted dignitaries as former Florida governor Reuben Askew, the mayor of Miami, a vice-president of the First National Bank of Chicago, and the president of the National Coalition of Cuban-Americans. Also in tow were a press spokesman, two photographers, a Latin American specialist from the State Department, and several men who taped everything and seemed to be in the business of gathering intelligence. Walter Mondale had intended to come, but with President Carter suddenly called to the Middle East to patch up differences between Egypt and Israel, it was an unwritten rule that he had to stay in Washington and mind the government. From the moment Mrs. Mondale stepped off the plane, she became the focus of all the ambivalent feelings that Brazilians have about North America, and the press did its best to make her commit some quotable gaffe that would betray our ignorance and indifference to Brazil and irritate the relations between the two countries, which were already somewhat strained. Two years earlier Brazilian-American relations had been the worst in their history. Geisel had just fired his minister of war and the second-highest-ranking general in the Army command in an effort to crack down on political torture, when a report came out in the United States that his record on human rights was poor. Brazil responded by immediately terminating all its military agreements with Washington. When Jimmy Carter came to Brasília in March 1978, his reception was cool and correct, but by carefully avoiding the subject of human rights, he smoothed the hackles considerably. Now, with the last Brazilian violation dated 1976, the Carter Administration was willing to drop the subject and to find more productive ways of relating to Brazil. Brazil, on its part, was tired of being treated as a miscreant minor. "The U.S. has always looked at the rest of America south of its border as a backyard, a source of primary material and a place to sell its machines," a Brazilian journalist told me. "But this country has come of age. It won't do any more to be condescending or exploitative." A high-ranking U.S. diplomat explained Washington's position: "We are trying to adjust to the new situation in the world, which is not changing as quickly in Brazil as it is elsewhere. From the time McKinley proclaimed it until 1975, we played the role of the world's policeman. But Vietnam was a turning point. Now we are trying to decide what role to play. The years since 1975 have been the first in three decades when we've been at peace, when we haven't had troops engaged somewhere in the world. We've changed, and Brazil has changed. Today Brazil is the tenth country in the world in political and economic influence. By the year two thousand it will probably be the sixth or seventh. It is already the leading third world country and the leading country in the Southern Hemisphere—more important than Australia or India—and it has just begun to play in the big-power ballgame. Washington wants to understand how it should relate to Brazil. Its specific weight, its straddling role between the third world and the leading trade countries, may be important in the new world order that is emerging. More important than Washington yet realizes.

With a small group of Brazilian journalists I attended a luncheon for Mrs. Mondale. Having tried to provoke her the day before into saying something inflammatory about human rights, the press was not allowed to question her directly, and we dined in a separate room with her spokesman, who immediately, as a precautionary measure, put everything he was going to say on "deep background." "Mrs. Mondale has been impressed with the vitality and the physical size of Brazil," he began. "I don't think most Americans realize what a big, vast country you have down here." Then he complimented Brasília. "Government towns have the reputation of being rather dull, but we've all been surprised." Then he assured the gathering that the United States had "no reluctance about accepting Brazil as a big and important country. We regard its emergence on the world scene as a healthy phenomenon and look forward to a bilateral relationship based on a consonance of philosophy about the kind of world order both our countries want to see." Then he took questions. The barrage of queries that followed was mostly about the U.S. attempt to prevent Brazil from acquiring the capacity to extract plutonium from the spent fuel of its new nuclear power plants. "It's not Brazil, a friend for more than one hundred and fifty years, that President Carter is worried about," the spokesman said. "It's having fifteen or twenty places where plutonium can be produced in the world." It was obvious that this explanation did not sit well with the Brazilian journalists, a restive lot, not one of whom was over thirty-five. They wanted the whole process to be performed on Brazilian soil, not so they could make bombs, but because to have attained nuclear self-sufficiency was a symbol that Brazil had arrived, that it, too, had reached the ultimate plane of technology. The possible hazards of nuclear power did not seem to be a factor for them, though a week later a journalist would make his way to the core of a nuclear reactor being assembled at Angara dos Reis, on the coast near Rio, without even being questioned, and the week after that, the accident at Three Mile Island, whose technology was the same as that of the Brazilian plant, would take place.

I left the luncheon wondering about the restiveness of the journalists. It wasn't really the plutonium that was bothering them, I decided. It was a kind of adolescent chafing, the malaise of a country that has imported another country's culture—lock, stock, and barrel, like the Slavophile movement that followed Russia's long infatuation with the civilizations of France and Germany. The Brazilians, like many people in the world, are in awe and at the same time, enviously resentful of American material culture. Teenage girls fantasize about men who are like Viscount Jackson of Nevada, the hero of an illustrated pulp novelette I found Bibi's children reading one day. Lovers go to places like Rock's Motel on the outskirts of Brasília, which boasts air conditioners and vibrating mattresses. Recently a law had to be passed to keep radio stations from playing nonstop disco music, which threatens to displace the native samba music, an incomparably finer sound by almost any criterion, as

and the envoys of twenty-two foreign countries had, already by nine o'clock, taken their seats. Looking up from the floor of the coliseum, where I had stationed myself near the podium, zoom lens at the ready, in a throng of photojournalists, I spotted Antonio Venâncio and his son José Nicodemos, Mrs. Mondale and her retinue, Dinah Silveira de Queiroz, Ambassador and Mrs. Gomis, the ambassador of Surinam, a chap by the name of Indirewe Seuradj Singh, with whom I had been playing tennis several times a week; and the envoy from Togo, its minister of education and scientific research, the honorable Boumbera Alassounoume. On the floor were the deputies, who had been sworn in the day before. I shook hands with one of the state of Rio de Janeiro's forty-six deputies, next to whom we had sat, a few evenings before, at a banquet in the Hotel Nacional for Elmo Farias, the outgoing governor of the Federal District. Farias had been one of the best two of Brasília's seven governors, the deputy had said. Now he was going to head up the national railroad commission. "A little activity on that front would be most welcome," the deputy had said. "In 1953 we had almost twenty-one-thousand miles of track. Now we have only nineteen." I shook hands with Admiral Montenegro, the naval commandant in Brasília, who was leaving to take charge of a fleet of destroyers and glad to be getting back to sea. I waved at the rector of the University of Brasília, a relatively calm and studious institution as Latin American universities go, with strong departments in tropical medicine, ecology, and anthropology. I smiled at Karlos Rischbieter, but not so broadly as to draw attention to the absence of my upper left central incisor, a casualty of *pêta* balls, a rock-hard confection of manioc, into which I had made the mistake of biting too hard a few days before. Across the aisle, in a brocaded white uniform, was General David Padilla, the head of the Bolivian junta, who had promised to step down as soon as a fresh attempt at democracy could be mounted. Beside him was President

Stroessner of Paraguay, the senior iron-handed dictator in South America.

Everyone stood up as Figueiredo walked down the aisle and ascended the podium with a half-dozen congressional leaders. A beautiful woman shouted down from the gallery, "Welcome, Mr. President," shattering protocol and clearing the air of unwanted solemnity. The papers later identified her as Katya Castelar, a Brazilian singer who had been living in Mexico for ten years. Then Figueiredo raised his hand and repeated the oath, and upon its conclusion a Marine band, wearing red jackets and pants, stood up in the gallery and played the delightful national anthem, which sounded like the overture of a light Italian opera. Then Figueiredo left the Chamber of Deputies and walked out of the building to the end of a ramp between two rows of dragoons who wore long jackboots and golden helmets and stood with their lances at parade rest. The Dragoons of Independence had been guarding the Brazilian head of state since 1808. Their present uniform had been designed in 1889. Their helmets were made of fiberglass. Figueiredo walked over to an old black Rolls-Royce and was driven the short distance to the Planalto Palace. There President Geisel waited to pass him the sash. The two men embraced. Geisel made a brief farewell speech, removed the sash—a green baldric with a yellow stripe down the middle—and put it on Figueiredo. Then President Figueiredo approached the microphones and gave his inaugural address. "I'll give him one thing: he has a good speechwriter," I heard a journalist who was reading a transcript of the address mutter to a colleague. The president swore that he would "make this country a true democracy"; that he would not rest "until the enjoyment of all human rights, as set forth in the constitution, is fully assured." He reaffirmed his commitment to provide suitable living conditions for all and to redistribute the fruits of labor "so that a few may not abound in what so many are lacking." He promised to combat inflation and to guide the country to economic self-sufficiency, so that its development would no longer be dependent on foreign financing. As he spoke, his words were projected by loudspeakers to a crowd of several thousand who were standing in front of the palace. For a moment, as I looked through the immense windows, the whole outer pageant seemed to become suffused in silence and slow motion: the Dragoons of Independence, now mounted, trotting purposefully past the crowd, the crowd waiting for its new president to come out on the ramp, a huge, billowing cloud (knowing that cloud taxonomy is one of the most subjective sciences, I will hesitantly call it as a *Cumulonimbus calvus)* framing the Monumental Sector, its sunlit edges barely holding still for a second. The city was full up: not a hotel room to be had, not a free parking space, not a hairdresser with a free appointment, not a tuxedo to be rented. I thought of Lelio's poem, "The Dream City." After apologizing for not having the gift of Homer to celebrate the new capital, Lelio quoted the words which Odysseus, still years from Ithaca and desperately homesick, speaks at sea:

> Green pasture, the herd, the vast prairie,
> Good laws, good judges, a blessed soil,
> And a happy people bending at their toil.

Epilogue

In the seven years since the publication of *The Capital of Hope*, a lot has happened in Brasília. There were two very important developments in 1985: the city became twenty-five years old, and the Federal District acquired a new governor, José Aparecido de Oliveira. A journalist and intellectual from Minas Gerais, José Aparecido had been that state's minister of culture in the government of Tancredo Neves, and when Tancredo was elected president of the Republic, he created the cabinet-level post of minister of culture and appointed José Aparecido to it, so that their successful collaboration could continue on the federal level. But twelve hours before he was to be inaugurated, Tancredo died, and his running mate José Sarnay ended up becoming the next president of the Republic. Sarnay and José Aparecido had been political compadres for thirty years, and after the interim governor of the Federal District, Ronaldo Costa Couto, was not confirmed by the Senate, Sarnay appointed José Aparecido to the office.

At the beginning of this year I was taken by José Aparecido's chief of social communications, Jose Sylvestre Gorgulho, to the Aguas Claras Palace to meet the governor. Several groups of people were also waiting to see him in the palace's reception room, which was large enough to contain several sofa-armchair ensembles and reminded me of Antonio Venancio's vast living room on the Lago. At last José Aparecido, who had flown up from Rio that morning and was not feeling well, appeared dressed in a bathrobe and pajamas, projecting warmth and humor as he moved animatedly from group to group, shaking hands and hearing out petitioners. Eventually he made his way to Gorgulho and me. We talked about the achievements that after only seven months in office had already made Aparecido the most popular governor in Brasília's history, and was winning him comparisons with Juscelino.

Aparecido's program, he explained, was to return to the original idea of Brasília, which had been to create an entirely new urban structure, one that would provide an alternative to the unjust, archaic social system that has been preventing Brazil from becoming a modern, democratic nation. When he took office, he discovered that after twenty-five years Brasília had lost track of its symbolic dimension. The rich were comfortably ensconced on the Lago, and the poor were out in the satellite cities, miles away, and the gulf between them had become even wider than in Brazil's older cities. Brasília had become a travesty of itself, and José Aparecido determined to straighten things out. He invited the triumvirate who had created the city—Niemeyer, Costa, and Burle-Marx—to come back and rectify the situation. Still lucid and dedicated, though now in their seventies and eighties, the triumvirate rose to the challenge. Niemeyer set himself up in an office in the Buriti Palace and launched an attack on the privatization by the rich of the city's public land. While the plan of Brasília explicitly gives the public access to the shore of Lake Paranoa, this access no longer existed, because the lots of the mansions on the Lagos Norte and Sul went right

210

down to the water. Niemeyer planned to give the lakeshore back to the people by putting in a bicycle path all the way around the lake, even if it meant displacing the *churrascarias*, or barbecue pits, in the backyards of the ambassadors' residences. An international furor erupted over the proposed bikeway, but in the end Niemeyer and Aparecido had their way. At the same time the governor clamped down on 170 illegal *loteamentos* that had invaded the capital's greenbelt. Many of the lots had ex-generals as their figureheads—the sort of *mordomia*, or cronyism, that has plagued the growth and development of Brasília which José Aparecido is dedicated to cleaning up. He was also trying to do something about the appalling shortages of housing, hospital beds, mass transport, and work opportunities in the satellite cities. "Every month," he told me, "eighteen thousand more people come here from the Northeast. The population of Taguatinga/Ceilandia is greater than that of five of the Northeast's eight capitals, yet there are only 149 beds in the hospital, shortages of surgical instruments, and eighty percent of the ambulances are falling apart." The main problem, he went on, is that the Federal District has been politically impotent since 1964. It has not had representatives in the National Congress, and its fate has been at the whim of federal politicians and appointees. But this was going to end later this year, José Aparecido assured me, with the election to the Congress of three senators and eight deputies from Brasília. Having filled me in on his program, Aparecido shook hands and moved on to the next group of petitioners, leaving me with the impression that the Capital of Hope is in good hands.

ABOUT THE AUTHOR

Alex Shoumatoff, a staff writer for *The New Yorker*, is the author of seven previous books, including *In Southern Light*, *Russian Blood*, and *African Madness* (also available from Vintage). He has an abiding interest in the Third World tropics and the relationship between man and nature. His most recent book is *The World Is Burning*. He is the father of two boys and now resides in Mexico City.